Advance Praise for *Secre[...]*
by Pete Briscoe and P[...]

"The secret (which unfortunately it is) th[...] [...] observe
the gift of 'rest' is urgently needed today. Pete and Patricia have given us
one of the most needed antidotes for our overly busy lives. Take time to
learn how to get off the treadmill. It will save your life."

— **Walter C. Kaiser Jr.**
President, Gordon-Conwell
Theological Seminary

"If you find yourself panting just to keep up on the treadmill we call *life*,
this book is for you! Briscoe and Hickman have unearthed the rare jewel of
rest, and present it to us in all its irresistible brilliance. Not to be missed!"

— **Angela Hunt**
Author of *The Debt*

"Hooray for my pastor, Pete Briscoe! He has discovered what I found out
many years ago. A balanced mixture of desire, ambition, dedication, hard
work, and *rest* can and will help you reach your goals in the sports world,
in your spiritual life, and all other pursuits."

— **Bruce Lietzke**
PGA Tour and Champions Tour
Veteran

"Just try to rationalize your too-busy-to-slow-down lifestyle after reading
Secrets from the Treadmill: Discover God's Rest in the Busyness of Life. It gave
me a soft God-jolt. The book makes clear, God says 'rest,' not just your
blood-pressure doctor! This is a great book with a timely message."

— **Marilyn Meberg**
Women of Faith core speaker, and
author of *Zippered Heart*

"Reading *Secrets from the Treadmill* did for me what the book encourages—
it made me relax and reflect. I learned years ago that I have to say no to the
great majority of things I'm asked to do, so I'm available to say yes to those
few God wants me to do. But I need to relearn that lesson periodically, and
Pete Briscoe and Patty Hickman helped me do that. Jesus calls upon us to
carry our crosses, yet paradoxically promises a light burden and rest for our
souls. If the burden's usually heavy and our souls aren't at rest . . . we're
missing something. This book will help you find what you're missing."

— **Randy Alcorn**
Author of *The Grace and Truth
Paradox* and *Safely Home*

"Stop, take a deep breath and read this book. My friend and fellow pastor Pete Briscoe and Patricia Hickman offer wise counsel for the weary and balance for every believer. You will learn the secrets of living in the soul-rest and strength of God's grace when you embrace the message of this much needed book."

— **Jack Graham**
Pastor, Prestonwood Baptist
Church

"*Secrets from the Treadmill* speaks a rare but essential word to our hurried, overcommitted generation. As a busy work-from-home mother of small children, I especially appreciated Briscoe and Hickman's call to rest and quiet. *Secrets from the Treadmill* has given me permission to do what's right for my soul!"

— **Marlo Schalesky**
Author of *Only the Wind Remembers* (Moody, 2003 Foreword Magazine Book of the Year Finalist), *Cry Freedom* (Crossway, 2000), *Freedom's Shadow* (Crossway. 2001), and *Empty Womb, Aching Heart* (Bethany House, 2001)

"*When will I find time to read it?* I wondered when *Secrets from the Treadmill* arrived. *I'm so weary*. But within the first paragraphs, as the sweet scent of a Shabbat rest drew me in, I knew this was not another how-to book but rather a 'God will' book. God *will* invite us into such a living rest—if we listen. God *will* give us the time and the way to find the peace He's promised. Peter Briscoe and Patty Hickman have not only brought words of rest to my harried soul, they've been the breath of the Holy Spirit telling me how to hear God's voice on the treadmill and given me the way to step off. They've shown me a way to share these Biblically inspired and personally lived words with others. A life-changing book."

— **Jane Kirkpatrick**
Licensed Clinical Social Worker and award-winning author of *A Simple Gift of Comfort* and *Hold Tight the Thread*

"*Secrets from the Treadmill* calls Christians to 'outrageous persistence' in the pursuit of quietness and stillness so that God's voice can be heard and His presence savored. It is a wise book for believers tyrannized by noise and activity. I was drawn into rest just by reading it.

> — Jan Winebrenner
> Author, *Intimate Faith* and *The Grace of Catastrophe*

"In Hebrew, Psalm 46:10 literally means "Be still and sink into the flame" of the Lord. Here is abook that helps us do just that. Filled with the cinematography of natures landscape juxtaposed against the true-to-life conflict that our fast-paced lives cast upon our spiritual well-being, Briscoe and Hickman invite us to embrace God's rest in our lives, and offer us a lyrical, practical guide to getting there."

> — Deborah Bedford
> Best-selling author of *The Story Jar, A Memory Like This, Just Between Us,* and *If I Had You*

"This book conveys the central message of the value of Sabbatical rest in the broadest biblical sense, as the subtitle suggests. Even more so, Pete Briscoe (my pastor) presents many ways to deepen one's relationship with the Father and one's own family in non-Pharisaical freedom."

> — Del Harris
> NBA Coach

"Pete Briscoe addresses a pressing need faced by every 21st century leader. His honest approach and thoughtful illustrations are a catalyst to personal growth in connecting with God at a deeper level."

> — Mike Duggins
> Associate U. S. Director, Campus Crusade for Christ

"If 'clean and reinstall' happens at conversion, and 'hard resets' on forced occasions, all Christians need '*soft* resets' to optimize life. The more I pursue life without soft resets, the more sluggish, complex, and performance-oriented I become. My pastor, Pete Briscoe, points us towards the Maker's instructions on resetting life, regularly and intentionally. Struggling but succeeding, he shares God's liberating strategies for measuring pace and making space for God in the normal, busy course of life."

> — Ramesh Richard, Ph.D. Th.D.,
> Professor,
> Dallas Theological Seminary
> President, *RREACH* International.

SECRETS FROM THE TREADMILL
Discover God's Rest in the Busyness of Life

Pete Briscoe and Patricia Hickman

NELSON BOOKS
A Division of Thomas Nelson Publishers
Since 1798

www.thomasnelson.com

Published in Nashville, Tennessee, by Thomas Nelson, Inc.

Scripture quotations noted NIV are taken from the HOLY BIBLE, NEW INTERNATIONAL VERSION®. Copyright© 1973,1978,1984 by International Bible Society. Used by permission of Zondervan Bible Publishing House. All rights reserved.

The "NIV" and "New International Version" trademarks are registered in the United States Patent and Trademark Office by International Bible Society. Use of either trademark requires the permission of International Bible Society.

Scripture quotations marked NKJV are taken from the New King James Version®. Copyright © 1982 by Thomas Nelson, Inc. Used by permission. All rights reserved.

Scripture quotations marked KJV are from the Holy Bible, King James Version.

Library of Congress Cataloging-in-Publication Data

Briscoe, Pete, 1963-
    Secrets from the treadmill : discover God's rest in the busyness of life / Pete Briscoe and Patricia Hickman.
      p. cm.
    ISBN 0-7852-6215-6 (pbk.)
    1. Rest—Religious aspects—Christianity. 2. Sabbath. I. Hickman, Patricia. II. Title.
BV4597.55.B75 2004
248.4—dc22   2004004211

Printed in the United States of America

04 05 06 07 08 PHX 7 6 5 4 3 2

Cameron, my blue-eyed wonder, Annika, my hazel-eyed princess, and Liam, my brown-eyed joy giver, my heart leaps when you walk in the room. May the Lord bless you and protect you, may the Lord's face radiate with joy because of you, may He show you His favor, show you His mercy, and grant you His rest. I love you.

DAD

Contents

Treadmills

The culture we have does not make people feel good about themselves. And you have to be strong enough to say if the culture doesn't work, don't buy it.

—MORRIE SCHWARTZ

Everybody today seems to be in such a terrible rush; anxious for greater developments and greater wishes and so on; so that children have very little time for their parents; parents have very little time for each other; and the home begins the disruption of the peace of the world.

—MOTHER TERESA

D ave, my accountability partner and friend, looked worn to the bone, wrung out. I had noticed that every time we got together for our once-a-week meeting, he appeared wearier than the last time we had met. His business, while prospering, had exacted so much of his time and personal energy that he sat slumped in front of me, weary-eyed. Even his words reflected the weight of stress that had straddled his life.

I said, "Dave, I've heard of businesspeople who needed a break, and so they just took the time off. Maybe you should take some time off." He stared at me as though I had spoken in a foreign tongue. Guys like us didn't admit to taking breaks.

"Take a sabbatical," I said.

Finally, he took the bait. The next time we met, he was a different person. He told me, "I'm finally taking a break. I just walked into the office, told everyone what they needed to do to fill my shoes, and then left." Dave took off for two and a half months. Over time, I watched in amazement as God refilled his tank. He said to me one day, "So, Pete, you look tired yourself. When are you taking your sabbatical?"

I went home and asked my wife, Libby, "Do I look tired? Do you think I need a rest too?" She nodded and affirmed what Dave had said.

For the first ten years as pastor of Bent Tree Bible Fellowship I had promised to take a break, promised my family and myself. But work—even God's work—kept me running, with my pace as constant as the changing minutes on my clock. I had convinced myself that stopping my work would kill the flow of progress I had worked so hard to create. Never mind the fatigue with which I lived. The very idea of a sabbath rest conflicted with my ideals that working for God was a nonstop mission.

Sabbath rest is a term foreign to our progressive thought. Yet we are drawn to such an idea, as though it were an exhibit in a museum, a masterwork we are not allowed to touch. We have rewritten God's design for humanity, which inherently contains a time for rest, and then called the rewriting of His architecture God-pleasing.

Having lived most of my life in overdrive, I had reached a point of dryness and exhaustion. Wisdom dictated that I take a two-month leave from the pulpit—a sabbath rest. It was a decision that opened a fresh stream of thought into the desert of my life.

When Anne Morrow Lindbergh penned her sabbatical's masterwork, *Gift from the Sea*, she scribbled with pencil and paper each morning of her summer break and then shared her awakenings with others. As she delved into her own soul, she began to understand that most men and women live in such a way that refilling their creative wells has to be a pursuit in and of itself:

But as I went on writing and simultaneously talking with other women, young and old, with different lives and experiences—

those who supported themselves, those who wished careers, mothers and those with more ease—I found that my point of view was not unique. In varying settings and under different forms, I discovered that many women, and men, too, were grappling with essentially the same questions as I, and were hungry to discuss and argue and hammer out possible answers. Even those whose lives had appeared to be ticking imperturbably, their smiling clock-faces were often trying, like me to evolve another rhythm with more creative pauses in it, more adjustment to their individual needs, and new and more alive relationships to themselves as well as others.[1]

The tide of life or, if intertwined with faith, the tide of our spiritual pursuits, has its own cycles: rolling in and out, searching, finding, observing, and leading us to act on our discoveries. We believe that acting on what we say is God's will or His plan for our lives is a natural part of servanthood. But if our only role is as active organisms, never reflecting or meditating on His ways, forgetting the feast set before us, then our energy is nothing but kinesis—movement in search of the next stimulant. I have known such Christians and watched as they bounced from popular movement to popular movement or cause to cause, never absorbing the beauty and splendor of the faith that they have embraced.

As a Christian leader, a husband, and a dad, I first had to notice my wrung-out life. Then I had to commence the refilling of my emptied-out existence. My spiritual source had to have a spigot, and I had to find it and then stretch myself beneath it. Like a thirsty boy beneath a garden faucet, I had to open my spiritual mouth and let the refreshment pour inside.

I had to seek a sabbath rest.

During this first sabbatical from the church, we used part of the time away to visit with friends. When our children, Cameron and Annika, begged to take a turn on a friend's treadmill, the oldest, Cameron, stepped on first. Within a short amount of time, he was running so fast I could scarcely see his legs. His sister watched him from the side, quiet—at rest. I looked at this picture: Cameron running as fast as he could go and Annika still and at rest, and I thought to myself, *Here is my life—Pete in North Dallas, and Pete on sabbatical.* Then it struck me—*They're both making the same amount of progress.* The Scripture came to me: "My heart is not proud, O LORD, my eyes are not haughty; I do not concern myself with great matters or things too wonderful for me. But I have stilled and quieted my soul" (Ps. 131:1–2).

Finally, I stood still long enough to hear God's thunderous whisper. The time had come for me to stop my running and working, and listen.

Before the industrial age, the majority of those living in the developed nations resided in rural communities—quiet hamlets that had church and family life at their centers. Human invention ushered in time-saving machinery that took humans farther and faster than any discoveries in the history of mankind. Our rural apex disappeared. But instead of using the sudden surplus of time for quiet meditation or introspective study—a practice that might have taken us collectively into the soul of our humanity—we applied our increased abundance of time to more work and a higher cost of living. Like Cameron, we leaped on the treadmill of commerce and progress, running faster and faster, but going nowhere in terms of our inner lives. The treadmill became our life. John Ortberg, in *The Life You've Always Wanted*, said:

> We buy anything that promises us the ability to hurry. The best-selling shampoo in the country rose to the top because it combined shampoo and conditioner in one step eliminating all of that time-consuming rinsing people once had to do . . . Many of us have "hurry sickness," haunted by the fear that there are not enough hours in the day to do what needs to be done. We read faster, we talk faster, and when we're listening to people we nod faster to encourage the talker to accelerate . . . We have largely

traded wisdom for information, depth for breadth. We want microwave maturity.[2]

Ortberg stuns us with this conclusion:

The greatest danger is not that we will renounce our faith, . . . but settle for a mediocre version of it. [3]

The Lesson of Shabbat

When I split open the word *sabbatical* and boiled it down to its root, I found the essence in its Hebrew meaning: "to cease and desist." Shabbat is a precept steeped in the first principle spoken over the earth's freshly drying creation:

By the seventh day God had finished the work he had been doing; so on the seventh day he rested from all his work. And God blessed the seventh day and made it holy, because on it he rested from all the work of creating that he had done. (Genesis 2:2–3)

In the portrayal of Creation, the Scriptures repeat three times that God rested on the third day. In the cadence of scriptural repetition, we can almost hear God's gentle pounding on the drum of our hearts—*take rest, take rest, take rest.*

The lesson of Shabbat whispers to us from the early shadows falling for the first time on virgin earth all the way through the loudness of our contemporary lives—*Stop your work so you can see Mine.* But rest in modern terms is associated with slackers. To deliberately seek a period of rest strikes a blow of guilt inside us colliding with a social mantra, one that enslaves us with a work ethic that is neither fruitful nor productive.

The great theologian Winnie the Pooh said, "Don't underestimate the value of doing nothing, of just going along listening to all the things you can't hear, and not bothering."

Stopping the voice that drives us to work without rest challenges our social fiber. We pander to the philosophy that rest is wrong. We buy into the opinion that a never-ending work cycle is a valuable ethic. We biblically justify that even Jesus violated the Sabbath. Yet while Christ's short visit to Earth created a role model for our daily living, we have to remember that He was the Lord of the Sabbath.

A mom once said to me, "I have to give structure to my children based on their level of maturity. But that does not mean I am bound by that same structure." By the same token, Jesus did not violate the Sabbath or disregard it to destroy its meaning but rather to declare His lordship. He had an infinite job to do and only three and a half years to accomplish it. Yet His pace, measured and slow, was not forced. He did not strong-arm His way into people's hearts, and He did not use a fast-bake method to mentor His disciples.

In the book of Mark, the apostles gathered around Jesus and reported to Him all they had done and taught. Then, because so many people were coming and going that they did not even have a chance to eat, He said to them, "Come with me by yourselves to a quiet place and get some rest" (6:31).

The Lord of the universe conveyed a core message through this one simple earthly act—man was not created for the Sabbath, but the Sabbath for man. While He dispelled the futility of legalism, He raised the importance of the need for physical renewal—rest in the midst of our passion-driven existence. *Work and then rest.* Somehow modern thought skips the latter, wrecking the cadence of Christ's acumen. So now we hear only part of the message, like a broken record that misses an entire beat. *Work . . . work . . .*

David Roper said, "Shabbat is not a day, it's a disposition, a profound conviction that God is working while we rest. It is rest from our labor, an unencumbered, unhurried, relaxed lifestyle." But our thought lives are shaped differently, and fitting this philosophy into a work-shaped ethic does not flex with what we've been taught.

When I finally stopped my work and quieted my soul, God spoke. He poured into me five life lessons that have become my continuous scaffold for meditation and a framework for seeking Him in still places.

The First Lesson of Shabbat: Rest and Know God's Reliability

The psalmist said, "Unless the LORD builds the house, its builders labor in vain. Unless the LORD watches over the city, the watchmen stand guard in vain. In vain you rise early and stay up late, toiling for food to eat—for he grants sleep to those he loves" (Ps. 127:1–2).

Here is where we, in our stubborn, silent aggression, disagree with our Maker. We cannot imagine God telling His people, "Relax a bit, and get some rest—I'll be watching, building." We do not notice how productive He was the first week that light and life spilled onto this earth, and then how He rested. The prophet of Chronicles said to David, "You will have a son who will be a man of peace and rest . . . He is the one who will build [the temple]" (1 Chron. 22:9–10). We forget God's plan yields more work through the lives of rested men and women.

The deeper message is sent to us in a whisper, straight from the heart of God: *Stop your work, and you'll realize how much you can trust Me.*

For the anxiety-laden majority, how is peace found in taking a sabbatical if the time is spent in worry that we are slackers? When we lay down our tools—our computers, the Internet, our handheld organizational devices—we imagine that all progress comes to a frightening halt. We envision cobwebs forming over our well-laid plans, dust collecting on our shining reputations.

The word *Shabbat* occurs in the biblical text for the first time when speaking of the miracle of manna, the mysterious food sent by God. Moses said:

> "This is what the LORD commanded: 'Tomorrow is to be a day
> of rest, a holy Sabbath to the LORD. So bake what you want to

bake and boil what you want to boil. Save whatever is left and keep it until morning.'" So they saved it until morning, as Moses commanded, and it did not stink or get maggots in it. "Eat it today," Moses said, "because today is a Sabbath to the LORD. You will not find any of it on the ground today. Six days you are to gather it, but on the seventh day, the Sabbath, there will not be any." (Exodus 16:23–26)

Even when they weren't gathering, his provision arrived.

But even when our excuse to work without rest is spiritually removed, we persist. Our work is our drug of choice, our escape from the pain of life. Work provides our significance. Even if our words proclaim that we trust in God, our actions prove that we are addicted to a speeding pace.

Is it arrogance on our part to assume that God in His boundless power cannot cause the world to spin without us? Or do we harbor a deeper worry—that we'll lose the control we've worked so hard to obtain?

The Second Lesson of Shabbat: Rest and Know God's Majesty

For me, a meaningful sabbatical incorporates beauty and tranquility and is more about drawing my thoughts into a rested, introspective state of mind and less about changing locations. But a change of scenery can take my heart places too long neglected, to show me things I could never see on fast-forward. To know God's majesty, I have to stop and recognize it: the things He put in front of me that show me glimpses of His greatness, His dignity, and His splendor.

The summer of my sabbatical, I visited Austria with my mother and father to minister together. We stayed at Schloss Klaus, the Capernwray Bible school, a college nestled in the valley between the foothills of the Alps. The river ran below, and the mountains filled the horizon. For two days we took leave of our work at the school to drive down the less-traveled roads, mountain paths that led us into villages greened by summer's breath. However cold the winters in Salzburg, the deciduous landscape had melted into an infinite eddy of life, beckoning us to explore the mountains' cache of streams and waterfalls. We wound through evergreen mountain slopes and blissful, snaking roads leading upward. We stopped by a lake for breakfast, and it was on this body of water that I drank in the beauty of God's amazing handiwork.

Psalm 29:4 says, "The voice of the LORD is powerful; the voice of the LORD is majestic."

I soon discovered that when I stopped and stilled my soul, I could then hear God and His majesty speaking from His creation. I heard it, that majestic voice, on a hike. One morning I got up early while the clouds hugged the mountain peaks. I hiked through a heavily wooded hillside until I found a clearing. The clouds partially cleared, and against the mountainous backdrop a single tree came into view. The tree towered above all else, isolated from the woody groves. Time had stripped the tree of its branches, yet the trunk had transcended the elements and remained steadfast and living, even though the wind had left it naked of bark. God's Spirit spoke to me and showed me myself as a tree, a leader in Christ's church.

By God's own hand, we leaders are pulled from the church by God and stripped of the safety of the crowd so that we are set apart for service. But often we feel the naked loneliness of leadership. In the quiet of the clearing I wept, realizing the pain of leadership. But welling inside of me also was the elation of an insider's secrets—of being able to see things first. That lonely tree had a great view. So do I. I realized that my Creator had shared a secret with me in the majesty of an Austrian wood. God renewed me and gave me a new resolve to bear with the challenges of leadership. That is when the remaining clouds disappeared, and suddenly the rocky cliff behind the tree grew visible. God's Spirit whispered, "I stand behind you, Pete. When you feel like the tree, remember the Rock!"

If I had merely *worked* while in Austria, I would have missed the entire majestic show—the whole voice-of-God thing: the solitary tree representing my life, and the towering rock face reminding me of the source of my strength—His Majesty.

The Third Lesson of Shabbat: Rest and Know God's Redemption

In the book of Deuteronomy, we find Moses and the Israelites camped on the plains of Moab. Moses tells the Israelites what God has told him: "Remember that you were slaves in Egypt . . . therefore . . . observe the Sabbath day" (Deut. 5:15). Israel's ancestors labored in chains for four hundred years, enslaved to Egyptian masters. No day off, no time away. God reminded them under the tent of blue skies that they were free and should take the occasion to reflect on their liberty. While God is speaking to the Israelites, He is giving us a picture of mankind's centuries of bondage to sin and how His Son, Jesus, stepped in to free us from years of roiling in darkness. God reminds us to stop and reflect on our redemption, and when we do, we are renewed.

This truth came alive to me as we traveled on to England to the Lake District and into a village of my ancestry, Bowness-on-Windermere. My father showed me the cottage on the lake where my great-grandfather was born and died. I drove by the dock where my great-grandfather once worked with his own fishing business. The beauty of Lake Windermere enveloped my senses, and my awareness of the past linked hands with my present. In the quiet of lapping waters and lilting sailboats, my heritage became tangible.

We drove through Kendal on our way back, both a birthplace and a resting place for our family. I was born in Kendal in the early 1960s. My father's parents, Stanley and Mary Briscoe, were buried there. We stopped to see their graves. What spiritual giants they had always been to me, imperfect people whose lives had been changed by one redemptive act—Christ's death on the cross! Stanley had died five years before my birth. Mary passed on fifteen years later. As I looked at my grandfather's simple, weather-beaten gravestone, I remembered the stories of his faithfulness and service in the local Plymouth Brethren church, how he had preached and pastored as a layman in his spare time.

Dismay appeared on my dad's face; Mary's gravestone had fallen over. Dense weeds had desecrated a matron's resting place. Dad stooped to right the marker but found it too heavy. We did not have gardening tools or anything handy that we could use to rake away the growth of weeds. The sight disturbed Dad, as though the resting place of his mother had been defiled. His mouth was drawn and his brow pinched, his vulnerability exposed. When I looked at him, I saw him all at once not as just a father, but as a son. It had never occurred to me that he was once a skinny English boy who grew up learning from life's hard lessons.

It came to me that the same words of correction I had heard growing up, had first been channeled through his life from the couple over whose graves he now stood. The same guidance and lessons of faith I now passed on to my children had started with two people who no longer walked the earth.

One of the elders in our church recently told me that on the way to work he often stops by a cemetery for his quiet time. He described the stark reality of mortality he finds there. I realized the utter truth of my own reality—that great men and women live for a short time and then are gone. Their gravestones fall into disrepair. (After several generations, they are forgotten except by those from a select group: the ones who lived a life of sacrifice that touched others with the news of their own need for redemption.) When your life is redeemed and your message is redemption, your story lives beyond the crumbling marker of your final resting place.

In the quiet shade of a family's resting place, God's message reached my heart. When we stop our work, God reveals how He has passed down the gift of redemption as a heritage that we can pass on to others.

The Fourth Lesson of Shabbat: Rest and Know God's Blessing

> The LORD said to Moses on Mount Sinai, "Speak to the Israelites and say to them: 'When you enter the land I am going to give you, the land itself must observe a sabbath to the LORD. For six years sow your fields, and for six years prune your vineyards and gather their crops. But in the seventh year the land is to have a sabbath of rest, a sabbath to the LORD'" . . .
>
> Before the Israelites could ask "How will we survive in the seventh year?" God answered, "I will send you such a blessing in the sixth year that the land will yield enough for three years." (Leviticus 25:1–4, 21)

Trusting God to bless us goes against the very grain of our works-ordered mentality. We fear that if we stop our work, the tide of rest will draw us under; the quiet of a peaceful sabbath will leave us stranded, hungry. When I stopped my work, I found a place where God could bless me and feed my soul.

From England we traveled on to Wisconsin, where we found trees stretching so high the first branch in sight was forty feet up. Over our heads a canopy of leaves spread from land to water, stretching green fingertips over luscious Pine Lake. With my children I watched the sun disappear behind the summer waters. We basked in the splendor of creation and the exuberance of sharing a sunset. Our communion of twilight taught us the intimate pleasure shared between the Creator and the creation.

We continued our journey to Spider Lake, and that is where I found my place of aloneness with God. Some people are not comfortable when alone with God. Perhaps it is, to them, like being alone in a room with a stranger. They struggle for something to say, shift uncomfortably, and then finally drift away to noisier places. But sharing intimacy with someone you know means that you can sit quietly, without words, and connect.

Very early one morning, I climbed up onto a lifeguard stand overlooking Spider Lake to observe the stillness of early light on the water. But a sudden flapping of wings broke through my reverie as two loons descended right in front of me. They minded their young, flying back and forth, noisily calling to one another in a loon's tremolo as they fed the nestlings. I felt the entire world disappear, as though I were the only privileged observer of the loons. It was then that I realized how God had made those clumsy, noisy creatures for my good pleasure, just as He had made us—His noisy, clumsy humans for His own pleasure.

In my aloneness, I met the God who allowed me to stumble into this world with all of my noisemakers and clanging cymbals, knowing that out of my quest for self I might also drown out the intimate music shared between us. God fed me and let me drink from His wondrous cup. When I quieted my soul, I drank in the joyous wonder of God's blessing.

The Fifth Lesson of Shabbat: Rest and Know God's Sanctification

God wanted the Israelites to know the importance of being set apart, a people chosen to demonstrate that God alone could make a person holy. "I gave them my Sabbaths as a sign between us, so they would know that I the LORD made them holy" (Ezek. 20:12).

When we toil at a constant pace, we might also begin to believe that through our works we are spinning our lives into a cleansing spray of holiness. We are not in and of ourselves holy. When we stop our work, we find that God alone is the bleach in our dirty laundry.

When I returned to North Dallas, I had to come down from my cloud and return to life in Texas. I wondered if God took a coffee break while making this part of the country. Without the majesty of mountains and beckoning lakes, beyond Austria, England, and Wisconsin, I found a simpler sabbath rest and the last lesson of Shabbat. Equally important are those brief, daily sabbaticals, the ones that force me to stop and look at the Godness that waits for me even in my own backyard.

I am not a yardman. I know yardmen—those guys in khaki

shorts that wander through the aisles of Home Depot, eyes gleaming as they gather yards of PVC for self-made automatic lawn sprinkler systems. But I do appreciate the peace and quiet of looking out over my backyard every morning while I gulp down breakfast. I appreciate beauty and therefore have to set apart places for beauty to thrive around our home.

But every paradise has its thorns. I had once planted an ugly bush on the otherwise lovely slope of our backyard. It was the Achilles' heel of my lawn, the hideous thing that I had to stare at every morning while I ate my breakfast. My wife assured me that when this unsightly shrub flowered, it would bring beauty to the scenery. But when the tangle of branches finally gave way to a lousy show of withering, unattractive blooms, I did what real yardmen do—I yanked it up by the roots.

At Home Depot, I selected the replacement—a showy hibiscus with bright pink blooms, a plant that could take the heat of a Dallas summer while providing us with a pleasant focal point. Within a day, I had my payoff. I journeyed out with my flashlight before dawn to see the first new blooms of morning. Three bright, open-faced flowers stood out like trumpets from the long stalk of plant. By the afternoon, the flowers had withered. But the next morning I looked out and once again, two more blooms had opened. The sight of it took my breath. I thought to myself, *A scientist could be given a year, and they could never replicate what God did in one day. God made three flowers for me yesterday. They died, so He made me some more.* The loveliness of His work renews itself each day, continuously. What was dead is replaced with fresh beauty.

I hung some flowering baskets around, greedy for more of the miraculous. Then I realized that I would have to water them—a task not truly pleasant to me. But as I took the time to tend the plants, the unexpected occurred. I found pleasure in the simplicity of a watering can. I observed the water trickling over the leaves and into the earth. It occurred to me that I hadn't ever stopped to observe the amazing construction of a

Virtually every luxury car commercial in the last quarter of the twentieth century has highlighted the ability of the driver to raise the pushbutton windows and screen out all the external sounds in the overly noisy environment. Yet, at the same time, manufacturers put in the finest radios then cassette players then compact disc players then cellular phones. Soon enough, autos will be equipped with computers, faxes, links to the World Wide Web . . . You can drive to the hills looking for solitude, but if you're not careful, you'll invite along as much noise and distraction as if you had pitched a pup tent in the middle of New York City's Grand Central Station.

—**Jeff Davidson,** *The Joy of Simple Living*

bloom. You can almost see the fingerprint of God in each delicate, clinging petal, and you wonder if the aroma might be the distant scent of heaven.

But more than that, I realized that because I had removed the ugly shrubbery from the landscape, the beauty of new life was now able to flourish. In the same manner, God removes the ugly things from a heart to replace them with the beauty of a life planted in His Son, Jesus Christ. When He removes the ugly, our lives are renewed, set apart—made holy. I am now privy to this information. A moment's sabbath spent in the backyard, and God breaks through—the light of life breaking through the deadness of my mental desert. I quieted my heart and found God's landscape pattern for sanctification.

It is not necessary to travel to Austria or England or even Wisconsin to find a sabbath rest. It is waiting for us in the places where we can be still and listen.

God said to the Israelites: "Remember the Sabbath day by keeping it holy . . . For in six days the LORD made the heavens and the earth, the sea, and all that is in them, but he rested on the seventh day" (Ex. 20:8, 11)—a day He declared holy.

It is the beckoning voice of God that says to us, "Stop doing for a moment. In fact, stop doing your job, your housework, your sports leagues, your newspaper, your Bible study, and even your ministry. Rest in Me—the source of your holiness."

We hear those words but yet struggle to grasp them. How can we find this sabbath rest, this still place where the voice of God becomes lucid to us, clear as the rain on the windowpane? We struggle as God's imperfect creation. I struggle. I do not desire another law that I most assuredly will break. And so my heart must find the answer to the question "Why must I seek a sabbath rest?" God answers out of His mercy.

The Quarrel Within

2

It is so easy to lose focus in the pursuit of the legitimate, even good things. Jobs, position, status, family, friends, security—these and many more can all too quickly become the center of attention.

—RICHARD J. FOSTER

In 1991 Eli Cohen directed a provocative film entitled *The Quarrel*. The scene is a park in Montreal, 1946. Hersh and Chaim, former friends and Holocaust survivors, accidentally meet, only to discover they have taken divergent paths in dealing with the atrocities they overcame as victimized Jews. One has become a writer and, fully embracing a secular mind-set, challenges his former friend, now a rabbi. The quarrel lasts for an agonizing eighty-eight minutes, as each man attempts in vain to convince the other that he has chosen the wrong path.

"How can you believe in a God that would allow the Holocaust?" one asks.

The other replies, "How can you live through the Holocaust and not?"

The plight of these two friends draws us into an argument that seems to propel the viewer toward some good purpose. But in the end, the audience is left with an empty finale and no solution.

Driving down a freeway, a man sees a sign for an adult bookstore at the next exit. A quarrel erupts within him—*Turn into this parking lot* wars against *Don't you dare park here.*

We stand bewildered in the valley of indecision. The quarrel within occurs in less obvious arenas too. Our struggle with our priorities creates inner tension. While we are still lying in bed, the alarm screams. The sun is not yet up, and the house is silent. We tell our bodies to pop out of bed and go for a jog before the family wakes up. But every fiber of our beings wants to remain planted under the cozy comforter. The battle rages. Many of us choose to supplant the jog and remain comfortably in the sheets. But others choose the hard thing and get out of bed.

When we think about incorporating rest into our lives, the quarrel commences—the desire to do what is right battling the will to do what has already become our pattern.

Adding to the quarrel is the culture around us, creating a completely different avenue of distractions that draw us away from a spiritual center. Culture is the graffiti on our walls, telling the world who we are and in so many ways making life easier, as long as we buy into its pitch. One of its pitches tells us how fast we must race to keep up.

John Eldredge wrote, "Adam and Eve set in motion a process in our hearts, a desperate grasping that can only be described as *addiction* . . . Addiction may seem too strong a term to some of you. The woman who is serving so faithfully at church—surely there is nothing wrong with that. And who can blame the man who stays long at the office to provide for his family?"[1]

We live in a culture of speed that has sold us a lifestyle that

> Brilliant people who should be masters of their appetites are at last managed by some dread fiend that was at first unwelcome in their lives. Then the fiend was made welcome. Then his presence was customary. Then he became habitual. At last, the addiction and not the Christian was master.
>
> —Calvin Miller

promises happiness yet delivers everything but that. "Do It Now" is a motto we buy in the form of desktop paperweights to remind us that we are running behind. Have you found yourself standing impatiently, waiting for your microwave oven to finish cooking? A dinner that would have taken our grandmothers three hours to prepare is now completed and ready to eat in four minutes, freezer to table. Companies invest millions of dollars in technology that will bring the cooking time down to two minutes. What will we do with the two minutes we save by upgrading to the new model?

Conventional wisdom says that we should work two minutes longer or rest two minutes longer. But instead, we add the minutes together throughout the week to play a few holes of golf or coach our daughter's basketball team. We confuse leisure time with rest. Recreation requires an enormous amount of energy to maintain. By default, free time becomes saturated with chores or leisure activities, robbing us of opportunities to enjoy a true sabbath rest.

Our perplexity allows us to continue along in the mainstream until we start to feel the weight of our choices dragging us to the bottom. Then, instead of pulling our lives out of the fray, we start to worry what others will think if we don't continue along with everyone else in the mainstream. Our patterns take root only to grow into dictators, those voices that take over our thought lives and sound a great deal like our friends and family members.

It is human nature to spend our hours in perception management. John Ortberg, in his book *The Life You've Always Wanted*, said:

> Sociologist George Herbert Mead wrote about what he called the "generalized other," the mental representation we carry inside ourselves of that group of people in whose judgment we measure our success or failure. Our sense of esteem and worth is largely wrapped up in their appraisal of our worth.

Our "generalized other" is a composite of all the Siskels and Eberts in our life whose thumbs up or thumbs down signal carries emotional weight with us.[2]

Part of the irony of the generalized other is that it is not really other at all—it is what we think others are thinking about us. The truth, of course, is that people seldom think of us at all. Almost everyone else is wondering what other people are thinking about him or her.

We worry about what people will think of us if we do take time to rest. While others may boast about getting by on four hours of sleep, or going three years without a vacation, they are rewarded with promotions at work and accolades from their peers. Meanwhile, coworkers notice when our workspaces are unoccupied while the rest of the team is working all day Saturday. We worry over the ramifications. I'm still prone to falling into this fear. Even as I write these pages I wonder what some of my hardworking friends will think.

In her book *Bird by Bird*, candid author Anne Lamott demonstrates to writers how to kick the voices out of our heads. Her advice to clear our thoughts of any domineering influences is well worth heeding:

> The other voices are banshees and drunken monkeys. They are the voices of anxiety, judgment, doom, guilt. Also, severe hypochondria. There may be a Nurse Ratched–like listing of things that must be done right this moment: foods that must come out of the freezer, appointments that must be canceled or made, hairs that must be tweezed . . . Then the phone rings and you look up at the ceiling with fury, summon every ounce of noblesse oblige, and answer the call politely, with maybe just the merest hint of irritation.[3]

It can be an enormous undertaking for even the strongest-willed leader to mentally evict those whom we allow to dictate our thoughts, in order to determine our own course of action. Lamott offers an exercise in mental housecleaning:

> Close your eyes and get quiet for a minute, until the chatter starts up. Then isolate one of the voices and imagine the person speaking as a mouse. Pick it up by the tail and drop it into a mason jar. Then isolate another voice, pick it up by the tail, drop it in a jar. And so on. Drop in any high-maintenance parental units, drop in any contractors, lawyers, colleagues, children, anyone who is whining in your head. Then put the lid on, and watch all these mouse people clawing at the glass, jabbering away . . . Then imagine that there is a volume control button on the bottle. Turn it up all the way for a minute, and listen to the stream of angry, neglected, guilt-mongering voices. Then turn it all the way down and watch the frantic mice lunge at the glass, trying to get to you . . . A friend of mine suggests opening the jar and shooting them all in the head. But I think he's a little angry, and I'm sure nothing like this would ever occur to you.[4]

Nor would it occur to me. But the fact is that Lamott is metaphorically corralling the frustrations of everyday life. To any average Joe or Joan, personalities take up residence in our psyches and rule at will until the hour we enter those busy mental portals and take over as the rightful landlord. God did, after all, give us the gift of free will, gratis. Imagining why is an exercise in mental discipline and offers us a whole new set of flying lessons.

A mother faces a boatload of guilt imagining her family suffering, motherless, while she takes a much-needed rest. She envisions her family's faces as she tries to explain her need for a get-away, while she believes her family is envisioning her lounging on a chaise longe, having grapes fed to her.

In her book *Intimate Faith*, Jan Winebrenner writes: "A newspaper columnist recently wrote about how she sometimes told 'white lies' to her children when they were young. 'Children aren't allowed in the store in the evenings,' she used to say as she hurried out of the house to the grocery store. She figured it was easier to lie than to deal with a child's tears if she told him, 'I just really want to be alone!'"[5]

A pastor fears asking for a sabbatical from his church leadership, convinced he might hear: "We don't get a sabbatical, why should you?" The pastor knows they work as hard as he does. When he finally musters the courage to plan for a real sabbath rest, he worries he will be perceived as a slacker.

Most of us play to a bigger audience than we should. We've heard the statement "I live for an audience of One," but most of our audiences could fill a hall. There's Mom and Dad (whether living or not), work peers, church leadership, spouse, friends, and bosses. We don't realize how their opinions dictate our lives until we take a step back to reflect. Of course, that luxury of reflection requires a little sabbath time, which we can't afford to invest.

John Eldredge resumed his topic on our everyday addictions by saying: "Remember, we will make an idol of anything, especially a good thing. So distant now from Eden, we are desperate for life, and we come to believe that we must arrange for it as best we can, or no one will. God must thwart us to save us."[6]

I had a conversation recently with a pastor friend of mine in which he shared with me what his life was like growing up. His father owned his own company and worked extremely hard. He would be out of the house in the morning when the kids woke up, home for dinner, and then back to the office until midnight, every day. Saturdays he drove the family to the lake house, drove back to work, and then returned to sleep with the family, so he could get up Sunday morning and drive into the office. Perhaps he lived in this high-pressure environment because his self-image painted him as indispensable. Most of us hang this painting in the gallery of our minds. We can't imagine our families, our churches, or our businesses surviving without us.

This was one of the reasons my friend mentioned in Chapter 1 waited so long to take a break. He, too, owned a business and brought in about 75 percent of sales himself. Although he had a strong team around him, he worked long hours and traveled extensively. His family suffered from his absence, and I could tell he was struggling, seeming more tired each time we met. Finally, I asked him if he could take a break. The company moved ahead full steam. Yet he resisted taking his hands off the wheel. One day the pain of exhaustion bore down like a thousand weights. He walked into his office, called his team together, and said, "I'm going to take a break. I'm exhausted; please pray for me. I'm not sure when I'll be back." Two and a half months later, he walked back into the office ready to work. He found a galvanized, confident team, and a stable and profitable business intact.

Pride is at the core of our feeling of indispensability. Pride says, "I am important," "I am more important," and "I am most important." God says, "A man's pride brings him low, but a man of lowly spirit gains honor" (Prov. 29:23).

If the U.S. government can survive without Abraham Lincoln, the L.A. Lakers without Magic Johnson, the U.S. Army without General Schwarzkopf, First Evangelical Free Church of Fullerton without Chuck Swindoll, cooking without Emeril, Chrysler without Lee Iacocca, the space program without Neil Armstrong, the missionary movement without C. T. Studd, the early church without Peter, and the church in Ephesus without Paul, then our corner of the world can, with much success, continue to spin in our absence.

Our various personality types, spiritual gifts, family background influences, and health and energy components dictate the way we manage our lives. This is true of the way we manage our spiritual lives as well. The largest contributor in the mixture is our spiritual temperament.

In Gary Thomas's book *Sacred Pathways*, he outlines nine different spiritual temperaments.[7] Some of them are more prone to enjoying rest, sabbath, meditation, or reflection than others. For example, if you happen to be wired as a *naturalist*, you are a person who expresses love to God in the midst of nature. If you are a *sensate*, you are a person who employs all the senses in personal worship. If you are an *ascetic*, you are a follower who longs to be in silence and solitude with God. If you are more prone to a *contemplative* personality, you are like Mary sitting at the feet of Jesus, listening and loving. An *intellectual* is adept at loving God with her mind, through reading and study. A *traditionalist* connects with God through ritual, symbolism, and ceremony.

However, the concept of rest will be much more appealing to you if you fit into any combination of these types, but less likely if you are one of the following types:

- An *activist* who loves God through active confrontation of evil

- A *caregiver* who loves God by loving others

- An *enthusiast* who is energized by celebration and demonstrative worship

In some church circles there seem to be less of the former group than the latter. In our churches we are surrounded by people who express love to God through the expenditure of energy. When we come together, we push and encourage one another to do more and more, and before long we find ourselves exhausted and spiritually dry.

Gary Thomas also said: "If we tend our garden, we'll have plenty of food with which to feed others. If we give our garden cursory attention we may have enough to just feed ourselves. If we completely neglect our garden we're going to be so hungry we'll become 'consumer Christians,' feeding off others."

One of the toughest lessons is learning that we can't simply float through life in the comfortable surroundings of our bent. Although God wired us to move and shake, that does not mean we are immune to dryness and weariness in our souls.

Franz Klamer is one of my heroes. I can still see him in my

mind's eye, careening down the downhill course during the Innsbruck Olympic Games. He skied with reckless abandon, nearly crashing on every turn, the adrenaline coursing through him as he crossed the finish line to win the gold. His drive energized anyone that watched. But he couldn't have maintained that pace for long. Without a stopping point, he would have tired or crashed.

Many of us receive accolades for our frantic lifestyles, not realizing that it is impossible to maintain the pace without crashing or weakening. The inner quarrel arises again and says, "You're not the type that needs a rest." God made some of us to be downhill skiers. But within our wondrous design, He created the need for rest.

Our inner quarrel is real and demoralizing. How do we resist these lies? How do we prioritize rest? For those of us reared with the good old pioneer work ethic, rest seems almost unnatural. Some would even argue it is unbiblical. Old lyrics like "Burn me out for Jesus" become our anthem. Pastors who never take a day off, or laypeople who serve as volunteers, surrendering an extra thirty hours a week on top of their paying jobs, often swallow the philosophy that leads to an unhealthy view of work.

We do not argue for a life of all rest. We're not even purporting a life of balance. We don't believe the Bible calls us to a balanced life—try to find one biblical character who lived one. We are not to rest seven days and trust God to pay the bills. Neither are we to work three and a half days and rest three and a half. God doesn't call us to a mathematically tidy life. God calls us to a life of imitation and rhythm.

If we misinterpret its meaning, one of the most terrifying passages in Scripture is Ephesians 5:1: "Be imitators of God, therefore, as dearly loved children." In the preceding context, Ephesians 4 outlines the lifestyle of the church, including a section that deals specifically with how we should treat one another. But to accomplish this list of challenging commands, we have to either lay down our human misconceptions or shrink faith down to some kind of physical feat over which we maintain control, whether through a juggling act or a stretching of our abilities. How can we do these things? Ephesians 5 provides a clue. Paul teaches us to live in the power of the Spirit. Sandwiched between these principles, Paul reduces the rules down to one simple, easy-to-read plan: "Live your life the way God does." But how does God live?

God Works Hard

I met my friends behind the dorm. We dusted off the Frisbees, slapped on the suntan oil, and celebrated the grateful end to finals week. The all-nighters had taken their toll, and the Mountain Dew consumption had reached unparalleled proportions. Our short-term memories had managed to supply our overwrought neurons with most of the crammed-in facts before shorting out entirely. Now we could relax for two weeks before the next term started.

Twenty years after graduating from college, I still compare feelings of relief to the ultimate high that followed finals week. The problem, of course, is that life is not like college. "Sundays come around with alarming regularity," my pastor friend said to me as I was beginning my ministry.

After finishing my Sunday responsibilities, I am already gearing up for the following week's sermon. But this is life, what is true, and our sabbath rest must meet reality, not fantasy. What is true is that we were made to work hard, but then to stop in our hot little tracks and let the hours pass without our constant input. What we discover is that God is still hard at work when we have stopped.

God's first act was to work, creating the universe, our world, the creatures, and mankind in six days flat. Genesis 2:2–3 says that He finished His work by the seventh day: "By the seventh day God had finished the work he had been doing; so on the seventh day he rested from all his work. And God blessed the seventh day and made it holy, because on it he rested from all the work of creating that he had done."

He went back to work the next day. Even with the work of creation accomplished, He still had centuries of fruitful work ahead of Him. As we travel through history with God's people, we observe His work of protection itinerant alongside deliverance and provision. (See Deuteronomy 11:1–7.)

Deliverance was seen primarily in the work of the second person of the Godhead as Jesus discussed His workmanlike view of the redemption process in John 4:34 and 5:17: "'My food,' said Jesus, 'is to do the will of him who sent me and to finish his work . . . My Father is always at his work to this very day, and I, too, am working.'"

Then Jesus handed the work to the third person in God, the One He called the Comforter. In the long marathon of faith, this passing of the baton was God's way of slipping invisibly into the imperfection of humans to finish the work Jesus had started. The time period between the ascension of Christ and the coming of the Comforter was a waiting room for the church. Acts 2 presents a picture of the disciples waiting and praying in an upstairs room. Between the time of Christ's work on Earth and the Holy Spirit's work done through us, the church waited.

Of course, in our present time frame, the Holy Spirit grabs His lunch box and heads off to work every day with a honey-do list of responsibilities long enough to weary a marathon runner. The Holy Spirit works every shift to move us closer to a love relationship with God.

Philip Yancey wrote:

> In some ways the Holy Spirit acts as a kind of "marriage counselor" between myself and God. The analogy may seem far-fetched, but remember the New Testament's words to describe the Spirit: Comforter, Counselor, Helper. The Spirit comforts in moments of distress, calms me in times of confusion, and overcomes my fears.

Consistently, the Bible presents the Spirit as the invisible inner force, the Go-Between God who assists us in relating to the transcendent Father.[8]

The work ethic demonstrated by the Spirit from the first blush of daylight throughout the endless tedium of night proves that the Creator of rest first created work.

He Rests Easy

God works hard, but He rests easy. "By the seventh day God had finished the work he had been doing; so on the seventh day he rested from all his work. And God blessed the seventh day and made it holy, because on it he rested from all the work of creating that he had done" (Gen. 2:2–3).

God worked, but He also rested. He did not feel guilty, wonder what people would think, worry about the world spinning out of control, or make excuses tied to His "personality type." He rested easy. God maintained the delicate balance of the universe while He rested, but He is God, and His work is continual. Nevertheless, He rested from His work of creation. When He came to a stopping point, He stopped.

So when God created mankind, He first told them to get to work.

God said, "Let us make man in our image, in our likeness, and let them rule over the fish of the sea and the birds of the air, over the livestock, over all the earth, and over all the creatures that move along the ground" (Gen. 1:26).

Then He modeled for them the need to take rest.

Remember the Sabbath day by keeping it holy. Six days you shall labor and do all your work, but the seventh day is a Sabbath to the LORD your God. On it you shall not do any work, neither you, nor your son or daughter, nor your manservant or maidservant, nor your animals, nor the alien within your gates. For in six days the LORD made the heavens and the earth, the sea, and all that is in them, but he rested on the seventh day. Therefore the LORD blessed the Sabbath day and made it holy. (Exodus 20:8–11)

He Created Our Cadence

Musicians have a time element that speaks to the cadence and rhythm of music within measures, such as four-four time or three-four time. There is a cadence to life too, something we might call "creation's six-one rhythm." God encouraged His people to rest after six days of heavy labor, staying in a rhythm that could enable them to stay healthy, productive, and connected to Him at the same time.

On a recent summer break I took a one-man kayak out onto the cold waters of Spider Lake. My son and his friend came along, each boy paddling his own boat. As I plunged the paddle into the water and pulled, the tiny boat whipped around in a circle until I paddled on the opposite side, thrusting the boat the other way. The wake I left behind resembled the trail of a drunk slug, weaving back and forth, making little progress. Observing the boys, I saw them each pulling lightly and pausing between pulls, perfecting a rhythm that produced a straight line. I soon mastered this technique and found myself gliding through the water.

Soon it was time to return to the beach, so I challenged the boys to a race. I gave them a head start and counted to thirty. But then I quickly reverted to my poor form and found myself losing ground. It's interesting how we can learn valuable lessons but then forget them when applying them in pressure-packed situations. Regaining the rhythm, I quickly passed the two boys, who, in their haste to win, were now going around in circles. Life, like a kayak ride, requires rhythm—not pulling too hard, and pausing between pulls—even when the pressure to perform is on.

A few days later, Cameron and I took out a two-man kayak

and had to learn how to paddle in rhythm together. If we got out of sync, our paddles would crash together in the lake water, hindering our progress and wetting us through. We quickly headed out toward the island and arrived sooner to its mossy shore than we had expected. As we circled around the back of the island and headed home, we realized what had rushed our trip. A strong wind hit us in the face on the return trip, one that we hadn't felt when it pressed against our backs. We had to work hard and had little time to rest lest we lose ground. We had to struggle and strain together in order to arrive home safely. But we always kept the rhythm.

Finding a cadence to our lives is easier on some days and a strain on others. But just as the soil and grass were formed and placed on earth for humans to find and use, so was the cadence of work and rest. Setting out to discover our cadence is as important as finding our footing when, as toddlers, we first discover the thrill of grass on bare feet. Our work-rest cadence is waiting to be discovered.

Work can be defined in various ways: employment, service at church or our children's schools, chores around the house, helping a neighbor move furniture, or volunteering at the local hospital or food pantry. God encourages us to fill our lives with work, and He sees the ability to work as a gift.

> Then I realized that it is good and proper for a man to eat and drink, and to find satisfaction in his toilsome labor under the sun during the few days of life God has given him—for this is his lot. (Ecclesiastes 5:18)

When God gives any man wealth and possessions, and enables him to enjoy them, to accept his lot and be happy in his work— this is a gift of God. However, when these things take center stage, that is when our hours are eaten away, consumed by the demands placed on us by the gods that our upbringing taught us were legitimate pursuits.

Wayne Muller once said, "What is at the center of your life? Carefully examine where you spend your attention, your time. Look at your appointment book, your daily schedule . . . this is what receives your care and attention—and by definition, your love."[9]

Rest and work share equal legitimacy. Once we integrate God's precepts into our work plans and understand His design for our rhythm, a Power beyond our abilities subdues the quarrel within. Once we hear this inward argument sizzle and sputter and finally die its well-deserved death, we may then venture out into the next part of our journey—the sabbatical of obedience.

The Sabbatical of Obedience

3

How do you get your soul to be silent? The mind never stops, does it? If it did, we'd be dead, so I'm not complaining. But how can we make it hush so we can hear God's voice?

—JAN WINEBRENNER, *INTIMATE FAITH*

I have a dear friend in our church who takes me out on Texas's vast lakes with an authentic fishing guide. To my delight, we catch hundreds of sand bass, filleting them, deep-frying them in the back of his truck, and then eating the delectable fish lifted fresh from the lake. Mike's "honey hole" (Texan for "a great fishing lake") is near the Oklahoma border. Recently, he included Cameron and Annika in our fishing excursion. Greedy for the large catfish, we poured a sour, rancid corn-feed mixture into the water near the dock. Waiting for the stink-loving bottom feeders to arrive, we put small hooks on the kids' lines and watched as they caught bream and bass. Without fail, the two of them pulled in fish after fish for twenty minutes or so until Cameron said to me, "Dad, I want to catch a big catfish now!"

I responded, "Honey, they aren't here yet. Just keep catching the smaller ones and be patient."

"No, Daddy, I really want to catch a big fish!"

"But they aren't here y—"

Cutting me off, he said, "I know, Daddy, but this is what I want to do!" So, we put the large hook and bobber on his line and threw it in the water right over the stink bait. Cameron watched his bobber floating quietly upon the glassy surface for three inactive hours. Meanwhile, Annika was pulling in fish by the basketfuls.

We say to God all the time: "I know, God . . . But . . . I want."

Dr. Scroggie was preaching once on the lordship of Jesus. A young woman approached him and said, "I really want to surrender fully to Christ, but I'm afraid He'll ask me to go to Africa as a missionary." Seeing the obvious struggle in her soul, he asked her to turn in her Bible to Acts 10:14. This is the story where God asked Peter to partake of animals that, up until then, the Jews had considered impure. Peter protested, "Surely not, Lord!"

A great work is made out of a combination of obedience and liberty.

—Nadia Boulanger

Scroggie pointed out those words to the young woman and explained that you can't say both of those things. You can say "surely not" when God asks you to do something, but then you cannot call Him Lord, for a Lord requires immediate and absolute obedience. You can, of course, say, "Lord," but then you won't say, "Surely not." Go home and cross out one or the other in your Bible. Cross out *Surely not*, and leave *Lord*, or cross out *Lord* and leave *Surely not*. Whether we say "I know, but . . ." or "Surely not . . . ," we are not surrendering to the lordship of Jesus.

Recently Libby and I visited a restaurant where we noticed a sign over the grill that read: "The answer is yes, now what's the question?" We have adopted this restaurant motto as a lordship statement in our home. When we think of sabbath rest, obedience lies at the core. God calls us to obey Him in these areas so that we can enjoy catching fish.

Jesus came and fulfilled the Jewish law, becoming the Law so that all paths from our obedience intersected through Him. Thus, when He told the people of Israel to keep the Sabbath holy, He was bypassing the old law and directing all new traffic straight through the grace of His heart. Paul said in Colossians 2:16 not to allow anyone to judge us if we choose not to keep the Sabbath. Obedience is not something we do to earn God's favor; obedience is something we cherish because we have God's favor. Obedience is a joyful way to communicate our love to Christ, and obedience in the area of sabbath will afford us great benefit.

Although the Hebrew word *shabbat* means "to cease," the English word *Sabbath* has come to mean "seventh." Thus Sabbatarians carefully observe the Sabbath rest on Saturday, the seventh day. Others, in accordance with the early church, feel comfortable observing the Sabbath on Sunday because it marks the day of the resurrection of Christ.

Growing up in England, I played often with my good friend Andy Thomas. One day my father approached us and said, "Whatever you do, do not go over the wall at the end of the yard." Andy and I had never noticed the wall at the end of the yard until my dad made it off-limits. Of course, as soon as he turned his head, we were gone. Over the wall we went, absolutely frolicking in our disobedience. Then I heard a deep, groaning grunt. "Andy, was that you?" I asked.

"I thought it was you," he replied.

We turned to see the biggest, nastiest bull on which we had ever laid eyes. He was not happy to find human offspring running freely in his field. He charged, head lowered and horns plowing toward us. I set two records for seven-year-olds that day—the forty-yard dash and the high jump. My sin nature prevalent, I found myself thinking, *I don't have to outrun the bull; I just have to outrun Andy!*

I cleared the wall and landed on the other side, only to come face-to-face with a more terrifying sight—my dad. His arms crossed, he deflated me with one look. He sat me down and said something I will never forget: "Pete, the reason I told you not to go over the wall was because I knew something waited on the other side that could hurt you!"

God intended that obedience would benefit us, not burden us! He designed the rules so that our lives could be better and more fulfilling. In Scripture, God asks us to do things because He knows what is best for us. Jesus tried to teach us a mind-set of obedience. On a few of those occasions, the topic of discussion was the Sabbath.

The Legalistic View

Even grace-filled, grace-giving Christians allow rules to blind us from the reality of Jesus. As I sat in the back corner of a small viewing room, I could not take my eyes from the screen as I, along with thirty ministers from the Dallas area, watched a pre-release of Mel Gibson's personal movie project *The Passion of the Christ*, a cinematic description of the last twelve hours of the life of Christ. The original period languages were used, the scenes pulsated with the tension leading to Christ's passion, and the dark hours were depicted with an intensity that placed me in the crux of God's last few riveting hours on earth.

The blood dripped; the pain was palpable. I watched with rapt attention as Judas lost his sanity, Mary wept silently, Peter ran for the hills, and Jesus poured out His life—literally. I wanted the execution to be over and done with, and wondered how long I would be forced to endure the brutal scenes that held me captive in a marathon of beatific suffering that is both an endurance test for the viewer and a powerful worship experience I cannot forget or regret.

As Jesus stumbled to the ground and Mary ran to give Him aid, she remembered a similar scene from His youth when, as His caring mother, she picked Him up and wiped the blood from His knees. Imagining it too, I cried. As she arrived on the ground with her grown son, she said, "I'm here." Through blood-smeared eyes He looks into the face of His mother and says, "See, mother, I make everything new!" Jesus finally arrived at the cross and we, the awestruck watchers, indulged in relief for Him, knowing the last trial will soon be over. He breathed His last while the screen went dark for about the length of time it takes to change into a clean shirt.

Then, the light peeked through as the gravestone was rolled away. Jesus unhurriedly walked out of the tomb as though He were on His way to visit a friend. No sentimental music, no flashy special effects, no dancing camels or four-hundred-voice choirs—just a real guy walking out of a graveyard. The credits rolled, the room was still, the lights came up, and Mel Gibson said, "Well, what do you think?"

I couldn't talk, so I sat and listened to my colleagues ask their scholarly questions. The first question was: "What will it be rated?"

Gibson, in his "guy's guy" fashion, explained that it would most likely be PG-13 or R, but he wasn't sure yet. Then one of the pastors said, "Well, I sure hope it isn't R-rated, because we draw a firm line in the sand for our people concerning R-rated movies, and it would be a shame for them to miss it."

A friend of mine, also a minister, spoke up: "But it is—as is most of the Bible—an R-rated story, isn't it?"

The discussion commenced as though someone had called to order a committee to argue the color of new church carpet. I sat in the back of the room, grieving that five minutes after watching the most authentic depiction of my Savior's death ever recorded on film, some considered that the next order of business was dissuading "our kind" from seeing it because of a rating letter attached to it. Corporate amnesia set in before the video equipment had cooled; the vision of the God-man, who died so we wouldn't have to be in bondage to rules anymore, was fading from our memories because we must first discuss the rules.

I sniff this out in my own heart and ponder if modern faith, with all of its Christian books, art, music, and telecelebrities, is turning sour on the spit.

I question at times if I am a Pharisee and, like my predecessors, am completely unaware of what is life-giving truth rather than what is a didactic exchange of ideas. Years ago my mom, Jill Briscoe, wrote a poem titled "The Pharisee in Me":

> Thoughts from Matthew 5:3–11
> One day I found within my heart
> Someone who'd been there from the start.
> A Prudish person—self appointed,
> Self-sufficient—self anointed.
> Though I, a true disciple be
> I've met the Pharisee in me!
>
> He passes people every day
> Who've lost their innocence in some way.
> He says a prayer for those poor fools,
> For breaking his religious rules
> "No time for mercy now," says he,
> "at Bible study I must be."
>
> And why should He the God of grace
> Be forced to live here face to face
> With him who hung him up to die
> Against an angry, anguished sky—
> Who pierced His feet and crowned His head,
> Who laughed, and left him very dead?
> Forgive me, Lord, Lord, I beg of Thee,
> Deal with the Pharisee in me![1]

The tragedy is, of course, that the Pharisees could have listened to Jesus and changed, but instead they ignored His heart-splitting words and continued to fashion a life around their misunderstandings. They didn't listen to Jesus, and sometimes we don't either—that is, listen to the Lord of the Sabbath.

John Mark described an amazing interaction between Christ and the religious leaders of the day: "One Sabbath Jesus was going through the grainfields, and as his disciples walked along, they began to pick some heads of grain. The Pharisees said to him, 'Look, why are they doing what is unlawful on the Sabbath?'" (Mark 2:23–24).

The Pharisees were the ancient equivalent of Joe Friday, policing the territory, observing Jewish commoners and expecting them to live lives commensurate with the lives of the priests in the temple. The word *Pharisee* means the "separated ones." They were a collection of Jewish leaders whose life focus was to fulfill Leviticus 19:1–2:

> The LORD said to Moses, "Speak to the entire assembly of Israel and say to them: 'Be holy because I, the LORD your God, am holy.'"

David Garland, in his fine commentary on the book of Mark, said: "The Pharisees represented an attitude that approached sin from the preventative side. They wanted to make and enforce rules that would safeguard people from becoming impure and immoral. Jesus represented an attitude that approached sin from the creative side, seeking to reclaim the impure and immoral."[2]

This distinction is imperative to understand in our present context. The law allowed people to pick grain from a neighbor's field as long as the hungry person didn't bring in the heavy machinery. "If you enter your neighbor's grainfield, you may pick kernels with your hands, but you must not put a sickle to his standing grain" (Deut. 23:25).

The Pharisees, however, constantly adding and at times nullifying the law, considered this type of harvesting as a violation of the Sabbath. Thus, to protect the sanctity of the Sabbath, they compiled lists of rules and restrictions in an attempt to quantify and qualify God's command: "Do not work . . ." An ancient Jewish writing called the Mishnah admitted: "The rules about the Sabbath . . . are as mountains hanging by a hair, for

Scripture is scanty and rules are many" (Mishnah Hagiga1:8).

When Henry Fielding sat down to write his novel *Tom Jones*, he gave the name Reverend Thwackums to the pastor, a name that when said out loud, summons pictures of the spiritual leader thumping the unruly children's knuckles. Reverend Thwackum's predecessors surrounded Jesus, and Thwackum's progeny populate our churches today. Jesus responded to the Thwackums that surrounded Him:

> Have you never read what David did when he and his companions were hungry and in need? In the days of Abiathar the high priest, he entered the house of God and ate the consecrated bread, which is lawful only for priests to eat. And he also gave some to his companions. (Mark 2:25–26)

Jesus reminded the teachers of the law about a remarkable day in the history of Israel's greatest king. The incident is recorded for us in 1 Samuel 21:1–6, but, when carefully read, it seems like a puzzling choice for Jesus to quote. If we read the text again to look for the reference to the Sabbath, we would be at a loss to find it. Apparently David's actions did not happen on the Sabbath. So why did Jesus use this story in His discussion concerning Sabbath restrictions?

Notice that David's actions happened with his men around him. He and his companions were hungry, and David gave nourishment to them. The connection between the Old Testament passage and the disciples' infringement of the Sabbath is found in the fact that in both instances, godly men did something that was forbidden. God did not condemn David for his actions. By relating this story, Jesus was saying to the religious leaders that their view of the Old Testament law was too narrow and was not in concert with the authorial intent of the passage. What did He intend to communicate when He wrote certain words? What does God intend to communicate when He gives certain commands?

Jesus condemned the Pharisees for their legalistic view of the

Sabbath. When we read the parallel passage in Matthew's gospel, we see an aspect of Jesus' response not recorded by Mark: "Haven't you read in the Law that on the Sabbath the priests in the temple desecrate the day and yet are innocent?" (Matt. 12:5)

The Levitical priests broke the Sabbath each week because the worship of God in the temple required them to work as they changed out the bread and offered sacrifices. This passage is a great encouragement to me as a pastor. My "day of rest" on Sunday begins around 6:00 A.M. and concludes around 8:30 P.M., with a four-hour break in the afternoon. Preaching four services hardly feels like rest to me, but I know I am in good company as the priests in the temple had to work on the Sabbath too. Even though they worked on the Sabbath, they were not punished because their responsibilities in the temple took precedence. In other words, the workings of the temple were an obvious exception to the Sabbath rules.

Then Jesus said, "I tell you that one greater than the temple is here" (Matt. 12:6). The "one greater" refers to Jesus Himself, the *new temple*. In the former days, people went to the temple to be with God. In the new kingdom, Jesus brings God to us. So, the argument goes, since the old temple took precedence over the Sabbath rules, the new temple does too. In Matthew's account, Jesus clearly enunciated God's intent in the Sabbath laws, and by doing so He gave us a long-term view.

The Long-Term View

I don't know where I got off track, but I thought buying a house meant that I owned it. After signing on the dotted line, I had an epiphany concerning ownership. First of all, I did not own the house, the bank did. Second, the house owned me, not the other way around. My first trip to Home Depot resulted in a two-hundred-dollar bill for hoses, nuts, bolts, fixtures, chalking, stain, cleaning solutions, shelving paper, and lightbulbs. My first day off after purchasing our home wasn't a day off at all, but a workday. Plowing the yard so that we could lay sod, painting walls, purchasing furniture, and building shelves in the garage sucked the life out of my rest. Subsequent days off have proved my original suspicion that slavery to my house is never-ending— the completed honey-do list is simply a prelude to next week's list. This ownership flip-flop happens with children, cars, lake houses, and youth sports leagues too. Things that we purchase in order to make our lives fuller actually end up owning us.

Richard Foster wrote:

It is important to understand that the modern counterculture is hardly an improvement. It is a superficial change in lifestyle without dealing seriously with the root problems of a consumer society . . . Courageously, we need to articulate new, more human ways to live. We should take exception to the modern psychosis that defines people by how much they can produce or what they earn.[3]

Our society has embraced this flip-flop of what we have control over versus what is controlling us. The Pharisees exercised a lifestyle flip-flop, too, when they rose up to enforce God's words as codifying entanglements. As Jesus explained the Sabbath to the Pharisees, He, revealing Himself as the new standard, reversed the flip-flop: "The Sabbath was made for man, not man for the Sabbath. So the Son of Man is Lord even of the Sabbath" (Mark 2:27–28).

Jesus is the new temple, the Son of Man, and the *Lord of the Sabbath*. That means the Sabbath regulations fall under His jurisdiction. He is more interested in people than rules, more interested in mercy than ritual. In other words, if they had understood the intent of the Sabbath law, they would not have corrected His disciples for picking some grain.

How often are we made to feel guilty for questioning popular tradition, and thus, allow it to rule over us? Madeleine L'Engle wrote:

Now we are often taught that it is unfaithful to question traditional religious beliefs, but I believe that we must question them continually—not God, not Christ, who are at the center of our lives as believers and creators—but what human beings say about God and about Christ; otherwise, like those of the church establishment of Galileo's day, we truly become God's frozen people. Galileo's discoveries did nothing whatsoever to change the nature of God; they threatened only man's rigid ideas of the nature of God.[4]

God intended the Sabbath to be a gift, an opportunity for people to take a break from the toil of life. Here in the body of a mortal, He peeled back the weathered interpretations of the religious to offer every traveler on the planet a better view of His love. For the Old Testament passages to be clamped onto humans like handcuffs, flies in the face of God's intent. The Sabbath was designed for us. We are not supposed to fit into the Sabbath any more than we are to serve and live inside that automobile parked out in the driveway. It is the same, Jesus says, as sewing an unshrunk patch on an old robe, or pouring new wine into old wineskins, a practice that would cause the bursting open of the wineskins and spilling out of the wine. (See Mark 2:21–22.)

The secret to the full life that Jesus wants to offer each one of us is incompatible with the way the Pharisees were telling people to live. We have to lope around the same obstacles, the ones painted with religious graffiti or social success mottoes. We cannot swap truth and light for dead practices, or loving obedience for legalism.

The foundational principle of the Sabbath as far as Jesus was concerned is that it is extraordinarily flexible. It was designed for us—for *me*. That means I need to determine the best way for me to find rest, solitude, connection with God, and peace of mind. When people ask me to explain how God's will works, I usually make the distinction between a tightrope and a playing field. People with the tightrope view presume there is one way to be in God's will in any given situation. Thus there is only one person each can marry, only one job each should take, only one house each can buy, and only one church each can attend. But that is reducing true spirituality to algebra when, in actuality, discerning God's will is much more dynamic and Spirit-led than that.

One of the great joys of the Christian faith is that it is a system predicated on freedom, like a soccer field. There are clear boundaries all the way around. It is wrong to go outside those boundaries, and there will be consequences if you do. But inside the out-of-bounds lines, there is a great playing area where we have the freedom to run, walk, fall down, kick, block, pass, or shoot. In the area of Sabbath rest, there is likewise great freedom within boundaries. To find the boundaries, we must remember what they are.

Your Walk with Christ

First, we find the highly defined boundary that says: *Look after your walk with Christ.*

Imagine this boundary as the difference between inbounds and out-of-bounds. Without intimacy with God, a prayer life, and the knowledge of God's Word, our faith is nothing but a practiced tradition. Like a marriage where the spouses cease to talk, a neglected faith walk will diminish, powerless. Imagine watching your daughter's team on a soccer field. Now in plain sight of all, imagine that boundary around the soccer field vanishing. The game would dissolve into chaos. The rules would be null and void as the players ran amok. When we look after our walk with Christ, the boundary appears all around us, defined by His unseen hand.

In *Mere Christianity*, C. S. Lewis spoke of tending after our faith:

You have to feed it and look after it: but always remember you are not making it, you are only keeping up a life you got from somewhere else . . . But even the best Christian that ever lived is not acting on his own steam—he is only nourishing or protecting a life he could never have acquired by his own efforts. And that has practical consequences. As long as the natural life is in your body, it will do a lot towards repairing that body. Cut it, and up to a point it will heal, as a dead body would not. A live body is not one that never gets hurt, but one that can to some extent repair itself. In the same way a Christian is not a man who never goes wrong, but a man who is enabled to repent and pick himself up and begin over again after each stumble—because the Christ-life is inside him, repairing him all the time, enabling him to repeat (in some degree) the kind of voluntary death which Christ Himself carried out.[5]

Our Worship Together

Second, we must remember to worship together. You might know some who have not practiced their faith long enough to develop a weekly relationship with other believers. If you saw the film *Castaway* with Tom Hanks as the island-bound FedEx employee Chuck, you probably remember that after his plane wreck, his hunger for human interaction was played out in his creation of a companion from a volleyball, aptly named Wilson.

Just as our design has an imbedded need for rest, we also have a built-in need for fellowship. Because of past pain or a fear of new situations, a person newly converted to the Christian faith may avoid church or Bible studies. Or they may not fully understand the benefit of accountability partners in the faith. We may not find them bunkered away playing thumbsies alone, but spiritually they could become castaways. When we remember to look after our walks with Christ and to fellowship with other believers, we find our lives all at once right in the middle of the game—whether we work or rest. By defining with spiritual boundaries our need for rest, we can maintain the focus needed so that we don't trample over the lines.

In the green grass between these two white lines you have freedom to worship on Friday night, go on a retreat, listen to some music—Bach to rock—read some poetry, take a week to hike through the mountains with your journal and Bible as your only companions, worship on Saturday night, sit and talk for hours in front of the fire, make a meal for a friend with a new baby, lie on a trampoline and look at the stars with your kids, or worship on Sunday morning.

As you consider what your Sabbath rest will look like, there are three factors to take into consideration:

1. You have true freedom to rest as you feel led.

2. There are certain purposes a sabbath is designed to achieve.

3. There are many different types of sabbaths in Scripture.

By following Christ's example of getting away, by discovering and prioritizing quiet time, by cherishing solitude, and by worshiping with our spiritual siblings consistently, we discover that obedience is designed for our sake, not God's.

My dad told me to avoid the wall because of the bull. My well-being was his primary concern. The wall is recognized when I walk with Christ. Every agenda is laid aside, and every legalistic claim is happily dodged when all traffic is directed through the avenue of Christ's gracious heart.

I can still see the silhouette of my dad's profile against the weeping willow trees that lined the driveway of our home in Brookfield, Wisconsin. It was my eighteenth birthday, and my dad was leaning against the car: "You're an adult now, Pete, and that means two things . . ." My dad, a brilliant preacher and outliner, would sometimes outline our conversations. "First of all, that means you need to start acting like an adult, and second, it means I need to start treating you like one. I am going to keep my end of the bargain; I trust you will keep yours."

I received my freedom that day—freedom from the family rules that had governed my life since the day of my birth, freedom from the fear of breaking one of them inadvertently, freedom from curfews, responsibilities, expectations, from the unsolicited advice that had marked my childhood, and even the discipline of my parents. "Never again will I give you advice unless you ask for it, Pete." And he's kept his promise.

An interesting thing happened that day I became free: I chose obedience. Now in my freedom, all the family principles that had been placed on me seemed sweet and reasonable. I craved my father's advice and often asked him for it. When I went away to college, I always had my father's words in the back of my mind, and I always wanted to please him. I chose obedience, most of the time, because I had been given the freedom to choose it for myself. I chose to follow the lessons I had learned as a boy because behind each one, I knew there was a loving parent who had my best interests in mind.

God gives us the freedom to obey Him in the Sabbath because He has our best interests in mind. That is enough to make us want to sit and listen to what else He has to say to us.

"The Better Thing"

The more comfortable we are with mystery in our journey,
the more rest we will know along the way.

—JOHN ELDREDGE

If knowing answers to life's questions is absolutely necessary
to you, then forget about the journey. You will never make it,
for this is a journey of unknowables—of unanswered questions, enigmas, incomprehensibles, and most of all, things
unfair.

—MADAME JEANNE GUYON

I was distracted. It was late, I was tired and almost home.
Fidgeting at the intersection, I observed the late-model sports
car careening toward the intersection at an alarming rate of speed
from the east. It turned north and, traveling too fast, almost
flipped over. Not knowing how to conduct a citizen's arrest, I sat
frustrated at the red light. Then, peering into my passenger-side
rearview mirror, I saw a police officer approaching on my right.
Wanting to share my exclusive information with him so he could
go and pull over the bad guy, I jammed my truck into reverse and
backed up. I was so distracted by the first motorist that I had
failed to see the teenage girl who had pulled up behind me in her
twenty-year-old car. Fortunately, her grill stopped my truck . . . for
an instant. Then it broke into dozens of pieces as I bashed in the
front of her car. The police officer put on his red lights and followed me to the gas station on the corner.

As I got out of my car to meet the Texas officer, all he could say was, "I can't wait to hear this one. What exactly were you thinking?" The problem, of course, was that I wasn't thinking. I was reacting to a situation that I thought required my involvement without thinking about the possible negative repercussions of my actions. We get distracted at times by altruistic opportunities that we think require our attention, but that in all actuality collide with our journey.

One of the reasons we struggle to find time to rest is because we are busy doing "the Lord's work." We long to be people of impact, to make a difference, and to leave behind a legacy. But the tyranny of the urgent steals precious minutes and fragments set-aside days.

As Jesus and his disciples were on their way, he came to a village where a woman named Martha opened her home to him. (Luke 10:38)

One day Jesus settled in for a meal at His friend Martha's house. Most likely He and the disciples would have reclined on pillows around a table, with their feet stretched out in front of them. Jesus started to teach as the women served the food. The disciples were tired and no doubt overwhelmed. Jesus had recently delivered the knockout blow, communicating how costly following Him would be. He sent out the seventy-two missionaries, giving them clear instructions that belied the struggles they would encounter on the way. Then He reminded them that being a disciple included going against cultural norms and sacrificing their own prestige and reputation in order to serve others. Now they had a chance to sit down, relax, and have a good home-cooked meal after being on the road.

I can imagine the eyes of the Twelve sneaking peeks into the kitchen as delicious smells floated through the air, that same air filled with the thunderous growling of fishermen's stomachs.

Martha's talents as a hostess perfumed the atmosphere. This occasion was cause for great celebration, fellowship, and, of course, the best possible meal for the King. Then the story takes a resounding turn. The scene demonstrates a social faux pas on the part of Martha's sister, Mary.

> She had a sister called Mary, who sat at the Lord's feet listening to what he said. (Luke 10:39)

Martha's sister, Mary, sat at the feet of Jesus. We use this phrase today the same way we say of God, "I'm resting in His arms" or "I'm walking with Him." It has become a metaphor for discipleship, and a pretty good one too. But for Mary it wasn't a metaphor, it was a "mat on the floor." She was literally sitting on the floor, right next to Jesus' feet, an act unheard of in ancient days.

The people who sat at a rabbi's feet were his disciples, his apprentices and learners. In that day women were considered somewhat like children, and many had no opportunity to study the Torah as the young men did. Jesus not only allowed Mary to assume the place of disciple, He strongly encouraged it and used her as an example for disciples through the ages. Jesus truly did release women from their social boundaries. He was the first liberator of women. Even though this aspect of the story would have stunned the early readers of the text, we must resist the temptation to miss the point of the story because we are excited about Jesus' attitude toward women.

> But Martha was distracted by all the preparations that had to be made. (Luke 10:40)

Martha is a picture of many of us today—distracted. The verb in the original language implies that the burden of her duties drew her away from time with Jesus. How many mornings have you sat down to read the Word, pray, meditate, or sing a worship chorus, and then the phone rings, the baby cries, the spouse calls out, the dishwasher breaks, the dog puddles on the carpet, the toddler colors on the wall, or the teenager misses the bus? These are simple life events that happen all the time, making quiet rest with God nearly impossible.

We add to these distractions Martha-type responsibilities—service, and work for those to whom we've committed—and the minutes are simply sucked out of the day, with no time to sit at the feet of Jesus. We do not condemn Martha as a bad woman. Nor do we call her irresponsible or a poor disciple. She is the ancient equivalent of the ladies at our churches who keep the cogs turning. Working disciples. Our churches would all run more smoothly with a few more Marthas around. Dinner that night would have run more smoothly had Mary been a Martha, but she wasn't. Jan Winebrenner wrote:

> I've grown in my understanding of God's unconditional love for me. I have come to value my time with him as one does a special date with an intimate friend. If circumstances get in the way of my private time with God, I can't wait to make time later in my day to be alone with him, to listen to him, talk to him, without distractions, without interruptions.[1]

And Jesus' words remind us that the ultimate value is not making certain that everything runs smoothly. The ultimate value is everyone knowing God intimately.

> She came to him and asked, "Lord, don't you care that my sister has left me to do the work by myself? Tell her to help me!" "Martha, Martha," the Lord answered, "you are worried and upset about many things." (Luke 10:40–41)

Martha was worried. That's what happens when duty pulls us away from *deity*. We worry that the potatoes will be just right, the disciples will have enough pillows, and the wine will be aged perfectly. If one person isn't happy, we aren't either. We worry that people will get bored before dinner ends. We imagine Martha's hope that Jesus would preach a "home run" so the party would be a rousing success.

We worry that our ministry is fruitful and the numbers bear out Holy Spirit success. If one person is unhappy, so are we. We work until anxiety is the biggest item on the menu, trying to make sure everyone has access to an environment of growth, while our souls die. Martha was also upset—upset that Mary wasn't helping enough. "She's got her head in the clouds while I have my hands in the suds!" she cried out to Jesus.

She looked down on Mary, not seeing her sister's spiritual focus, and considered her impractical. Modern-day disciples that take sabbath rest to heart are often described with similar phraseology. "Martha, Martha," Christ responded. We do not know His tone but can only imagine. Whether He reprimanded, comforted, or taught her, we'll never really know. Jesus' response teaches us three important principles about sabbath rest.

Listening to Jesus Is More Important Than Serving Jesus

"Martha, Martha," the Lord answered, "you are worried and upset about many things, but only one thing is needed." (Luke 10:41–42)

"Only one thing is needed," Jesus said. Sitting at His feet to listen is the necessary component to the life of discipleship. Think about it for a while—God doesn't really need us to work for Him. Serving benefits us as we exercise our flight into humility (see Philippians 2:3–4). Sitting in a church service and hearing Brother Bob stand and make the annual children's ministry announcement might cause us to think otherwise: "Dear brothers and sisters, our kids need you! We don't care if you can teach, if you like kids, or if you can even read, to be completely honest! If you have a heartbeat, children's ministry is the place for you! Our services will be overrun with attention-grabbing, communion-tray-grabbing, hymnal-grabbing, toupee-grabbing toddlers if some of you consumer-focused pew sitters don't get involved. We'll have to close classes if you don't sign up! God needs you!"

I was twenty-eight years old when I started preaching every week. I was the new pastor of a church in Dallas, learning on the job. After I finished a sermon, people would come up and say, "Wow, Pete, that was great. How are you going to top that one next week?"

I knew better than to say, "It wasn't me; it was God" because my dad had told me of an occasion when he had said that, only to hear from the woman complimenting him: "It wasn't *that* good!"

As the subsequent weeks wore on, I would find myself working diligently on my sermons, hoping to top the last week's offering. Libby would call me at church on Saturday evening, asking what time I was coming home. I would try to make it by midnight but many times failed. I would grab three hours of sleep and then drive back to the office to finish. I would be disappointed each week when 9:00 A.M. arrived because I was convinced that if I had another hour, I could polish the message more fully.

Libby eventually challenged the motives behind my diligence. She wondered out loud if pride was driving my sermon preparation and asked if I thought I could maintain this pace long-term. Externally struggling with her words, internally agreeing, I made a commitment to finish my sermon preparation by Friday at 5:00 P.M.

The next week was terrifying. I left the office at five o'clock on Friday with a partial sermon and a stomachache. I dragged my body out of bed on Sunday morning and went to the office and prayed: "Jesus, this is Your church and Your sermon. I am trying to do the right thing, and I'm scared this sermon is going to bomb. But this is Your church, You love her more than I do, and You also value my health and a pure heart. So, take this sermon and make something out of it." It wasn't the best sermon I had ever preached, but it certainly wasn't my worst.

Recently I arrived at church at four o'clock on Sunday morning without a sermon. I had been out late at meetings the entire week, and for the first time in my life had had no preparation time. My topic was "A Letter to the Church in America from Jesus," the last in a series of messages from the letters to the churches in Revelation 2–3.

The Holy Spirit whispered to my pliable heart: "Just read the text." I read through the Gospels, asking the Spirit to point out the specific passages Jesus wanted to say to our church. I wrote those passages down, put them into the form of a letter, and stood up in front of our body and read Scripture to them for forty minutes. To rest in His sufficiency, for me, was to find a new rest— out of my control and completely dependent on Him.

To take the legs out from under our annual recruitment announcements: *God doesn't need us*. When He calls us to service, it is for a multitude of reasons that may or may not be fully revealed to us on this side of life. This obviously goes without saying, but when it isn't said, we live as though it isn't true. Work is a gift from God to us, not our gift of gratitude to Him. As far as He is concerned, two things are necessary: sitting and listening.

> The results of really taking seriously the command to listen can be surprising. Passages we thought we knew by heart speak to us in a whole new way.
>
> —**Michael Card**, *Scribblings in the Sand*

So how do we sit at Jesus' feet today? He isn't here physically any longer, so to accomplish this feat pragmatically, we have to face that we are *quiet-time challenged*. When I admit that to people, they share with great relief their own struggles to have a consistent quiet time. Come October, guilty feelings abound for missing a day—back in February—of our "read through the Bible in a year" checklist. We know we have been redeemed that we might be free, but the law seems to creep back into our lives in religious rituals such as "the quiet time," a phrase found nowhere in Scripture. (See Galatians 5:1.) I am not recommending that we stop having quiet times; I am suggesting that we perceive the concept through narrow windows. A quiet time is not an opportunity to check off one more duty to please our deity. A quiet time is an opportunity to sit at the feet of Jesus and soak.

In his challenging book *The Scandal of the Evangelical Mind*, Mark Noll discussed the "two books" of God. One we call "general revelation," where God writes His message to us in nature. In Paul's diatribe against mankind in Romans 1, he reminded us that there is enough knowledge about God to be found in nature as to make people culpable for their rejection of Him.

David painted a magnificent picture of God's megaphone called nature:

The heavens *declare* the glory of God;
 the skies *proclaim* the work of his hands.
Day after day they *pour forth speech;*
 night after night they *display* knowledge.
There is no speech or language
 where their voice is not heard.
Their *voice* goes out into all the earth,
 their *words* to the ends of the world. (Psalm 19:1—4, italics added)

There seems to be a growing animosity between the evangelical world and the scientific community. We need to remember that scientists are simply the exegetes of God's "first book." They are trying to understand this amazing work of art called creation. Like some exegetes of Scripture, some are bad at it, others are ignorant of it, and still some are fighting against it. However, enjoying a vista of mountains, listening to the curl of the surf, watching a cheetah gracefully speed across the Serengeti Plain, snuggling with our children during a thunderstorm, or walking through a field of bluebonnets can actually be an opportunity to sit at the feet of the master Creator Himself—Jesus.

Through him [Jesus] all things were made; without him nothing was made that has been made. (John 1:3)

My wife, Libby, and I were recently at a pastors' conference that ran simultaneously with a conference for the "emerging church." This group was discussing the best way to reach a generation of young people who have been turned off by traditional churches. Their worship service was a sensory overload, with six video screens running various images on different walls through the entire energizing event. We loved to see the dynamic and radical faith of hundreds of young people brazenly committed to reaching their world for Christ. After the session Libby, who is a physician assistant and loves the scientific world, asked me if I had watched the black-and-white video of the cells splitting. I sheepishly admitted that I had seen it but spent much of my time watching the *Mr. T* video on the next screen. After rolling her eyes, she said, "That cell splitting was incredible! I couldn't take my eyes off it!"

She reminded me of the unfathomable and intricate balance that God has placed in each person so that life can continue from one moment to the next. As Libby continued, it struck me that she was describing a powerful worship event that she had just experienced. As she observed one small aspect of God's "first book," she was overwhelmed with praise for His magnanimous creation!

But creation is only "book one" in God's two-part series. It can teach us about God's eternal power and divine nature, but the whole story of mankind and God's relationship to us is found in His "special revelation." David continued:

The law of the LORD is perfect,
  reviving the soul.
The statutes of the LORD are trustworthy,
  making wise the simple.
The precepts of the LORD are right,
  giving joy to the heart.
The commands of the LORD are radiant,
  giving light to the eyes.
The fear of the LORD is pure,
  enduring forever.
The ordinances of the LORD are sure
  and altogether righteous.
They are more precious than gold,
  than much pure gold;
they are sweeter than honey,
  than honey from the comb.
By them is your servant warned;
  in keeping them there is great reward. (PSALM 19:7–11)

Look at the promises in His "second book" available to those who sit at the feet of Jesus. We will be revived, wise, joyful, and by reading it, we will have light for our eyes and warnings of danger and reward. Scripture is described as trustworthy, perfect, right, radiant, sure, and altogether righteous. This book is more life-giving than anything we can imagine. David spent an enormous amount of time outside reading and writing God's Word, and as a result had a clear picture of God's "two books"!

If we prioritize sabbath time, we are wise to follow David's example. When we get outside with a Bible to feel the sun on our shoulders and the grass between our toes, God is revealed. By reading God's special revelation while we sit in His general revelation, chances are good He will reveal Himself to us. We can be counted among the privileged who say that they have heard from God.

We Have to Say No in Order to Say Yes

I have concluded that the greatest enemy of rest is sleep. Sabbath rest usually occurs at times when other people are sleeping. Growing up, I often heard my mother saying, "I'd rather go without sleep than without Jesus" or my dad instructing, "Never my head on the pillow lest my nose has been in the book."

Abundant sleep is one of the luxuries that we forfeit in order to spiritually rest. But it is only one of them.

Mary has chosen what is better, and it will not be taken away from her. (Luke 10:42)

Mary had to *choose* to sit at Jesus' feet. It took a conscious decision and a willful rejection of the other options available to her.

While in seminary, one of my professors said to me, "Remember, every time you say yes to something outside your normal job description, you are saying no to someone you love." He was aware that by definition, the job description of a pastor requires the necessity of "dropping everything" to go and serve. But his point was well taken. We only have so much time in which to shape our work. When we say yes to something, we're automatically saying no to something else. We have to make conscious decisions to say no to worthwhile opportunities in order to keep the pace of our lives at a healthy rhythm.

One morning I met with a member of my staff and assigned him an additional job. The next day he came in and sat down at my desk to present a pie graph on a piece of paper. It was segmented into his work responsibilities. He said, "Pete, you know I am absolutely committed to this body and my calling here. I have X number of hours to invest in my ministry, and this is how those hours are now assigned." He proceeded to show me the pie graph. "Which one of these things would you like me to drop," he asked, "so I can fulfill the new responsibility with excellence?"

In one simple drawing, he showed me the reality of my request. Part of my job as a senior pastor is to limit the number and types of meetings I will have with parishioners who are struggling with crises in their lives. This has been so difficult for me because I am a pleaser and a pastor; I enjoy helping people and hate the thought of people being disappointed in me—and yes, I know how dysfunctional that sounds.

It became apparent to me, however, that I had no time to read, study, or pray because I was meeting with people all the time. I pulled in Tim, one of the associate pastors, and asked if he would be willing to expand his responsibilities to care for the hurting people who want to come in and see me. This was a win-win situation because Tim's giftedness is in the pastoral care area and mine is not. Tim's ministry in the lives of these people has taken off, and he is exercising his gift in a remarkable way. I continue to encourage people to meet with Tim instead of setting appointments with me, and as I say no, I am able to say yes to sitting at Jesus' feet.

Notice also that Mary chose what is "better." This is a comparative statement between two good things, not between a good and a bad. Serving Jesus is obviously a wonderful thing to do, unless it takes us away from Jesus. Then sitting at His feet is considered a better choice. We do not advocate sitting all the time or serving all the time. We encourage finding the perfect rhythm.

One evening I returned for our night services on a hot August Sunday with all three kids in my car. I was mentally focused on the sermon I had already preached twice that morning but found myself gearing up once more for a go at the pulpit. We parked and walked through the large parking lot, making sure that cars didn't run over us as we hurried inside to escape the Dallas heat. We got inside the children's building and walked over to the wall where the children's nametags were posted. I pressed Cameron's nametag onto his shirt, stuck Annika's to her blouse, and asked, "Where's Liam?" Neither Cameron nor Annika had any idea, so I quickly looked around the lobby but couldn't see him anywhere. I tried to remember the last time I had seen him, and that's when it occurred to me that I had never taken him out of his car seat. Four minutes had passed; the car interior was probably 120 degrees by now.

I left the older kids with a friend and sprinted to the back of the parking lot, arriving at the car to find Liam screaming and covered in sweat, still strapped into the backseat. I pulled him out, held him close to my body, and wept. Children die in our southwestern climate because parents get distracted and leave them in cars. I was distracted by something as good as a sermon, but it could have cost me something much more precious—my youngest son.

It is possible to be distracted by something good, which causes us to miss something better. I check the car two or three times each time I leave it now to make sure all my children are accounted for. It took a jolt of adrenaline, a sense of grief and loss, and a debilitating experience of failure to catch my attention.

However, it would be foolish for me to stop preaching because I forgot and left Liam in the car. The message is not that we should stop our work altogether, lay down the plow, or forsake our duties. Daily we see people who have completely shut down and stopped contributing. They are the men and women standing at the city intersections with cardboard signs that read, "Will work for food." We don't stop serving in order to rest. We live in the rhythm of service and rest.

God used nature to remind us that rest and productivity—sitting and serving—form a healthy rhythm.

The LORD said to Moses on Mount Sinai, "Speak to the Israelites and say to them: 'When you enter the land I am going to give you, the land itself must observe a sabbath to the LORD. For six years sow your fields, and for six years prune your vineyards and gather their crops. But in the seventh year the land is to have a sabbath of rest, a sabbath to the LORD. Do not sow your fields or prune your vineyards. Do not reap what grows of itself or harvest the grapes of your untended vines. The land is to have a year of rest. (Leviticus 25:1–5)

The cycle of celebrations for the nation of Israel centered around the sabbath concept. First of all, they were to rest on the seventh day. They were also instructed to set the seventh year apart as a special time. God said to let the fields rest too. Of course, the first thought that pops into our heads is: *What did they eat?* God anticipated that the people of Israel would ask the same question:

> You may ask, "What will we eat in the seventh year if we do not plant or harvest our crops?" I will send you such a blessing in the sixth year that the land will yield enough for three years. While you plant during the eighth year, you will eat from the old crop and will continue to eat from it until the harvest of the ninth year comes in. (Leviticus 25:20–22)

God provides fruit in abundance while we cannot. And His master plan is to provide fruit to those who grasp the cycle of work and rest. As with the Israelites, He provides it not only up front but afterward.

The seventh month each year was set aside as a special month too. On the first day of the month no work was to be done, and the Feast of Trumpets was held. The tenth day was the Day of Atonement, a crucial event in salvation history, and a day where no work was allowed. On the fifteenth day, while no normal work was allowed, the Feast of Tabernacles began, lasting seven days. It is this feast that provides the backdrop for our next lesson in sabbath rest (see Numbers 29).

Rivers, Trees, and Me

Thirsty hearts are those whose longings have been wakened by the touch of God within them.

—A. W. TOZER

Not everyone turns to God in a time of need, of course. Yet whenever I sense a thirst, a restlessness, I have hope for new life, the Creator's specialty.

—PHILIP YANCEY

No water, no crops. No crops, no food. No food, no life. During Christ's time on the earth, water epitomized the cultural symbol of prosperity. The sight of a summer shower spoke of sustenance and the continuance of life. As a result, many ancient cultures worshiped the gods of water—Babylonia's Ea, Acadia's Apsu, Persia's Apam Napat, and the Aztecs' Chalchiuhtlicue. But in Israel, the people knew that Yahweh was the God who brought water, and they celebrated this provision and pleaded for its continuance through ceremony.

The sun was rising, lifting to face Jerusalem like a golden mirror. Early in the morning the temple priests gathered in a processional and walked toward the Pool of Siloam, where they dipped their golden pitchers into the water. They arrived at the water gate upon their return to the temple. Three trumpets sounded to inaugurate joyful cries from the hordes of people filling the temple grounds. The temple choir rolled out a merry outpouring of praise to God that led the festival-goers to jubilant heights. The priests circled the altar, paused, and then poured out the water onto the altar. At the priest's signal of a raised hand, the festivities came to an end.

This ritual took place daily during the seven-day Feast of the Tabernacles, and then seven times on the last day. The reading of Scripture also prevailed during the feast. Every day the priests read aloud the same three passages. One passage looked back to God's provision for the people of Israel when, after a time of wandering in the wilderness, they had run out of water. The people threatened Moses, who in turn complained to God. God instructed Moses to strike the rock at Horeb, where life-giving water flowed (see Exodus 17:6).

Every day the priests reached down into the Pool of Siloam as a reminder to the people of this great miracle of God. But the two other passages read by the priests during the feast both looked to the future—the "Day of the Lord"—instead of to the past.

> On that day living water will flow out from Jerusalem, half to the eastern sea and half to the western sea, in summer and in winter. (Zechariah 14:8)

A prophecy from Ezekiel 47 develops the sketch of Zechariah into a full-blown painting. In this vision, a "man" takes Ezekiel to the temple, where he sees a river flowing from the foundation. The river grows in size, depth, and intensity until it is no longer safe to cross. "When I arrived there, I saw a great number of trees on each side of the river. He said to me, 'This water flows toward the eastern region and goes down into the Arabah, where it enters the Sea'" (Ezek. 47:7–8).

The "Sea" is the Dead Sea, and the Arabah is the desert that surrounds it. The Dead Sea is dead because of the incredibly high sodium and mineral content of the water. While on a trip to Israel, I swam in the Dead Sea. When I walked out, my body felt slick, oil-coated. I found out why. The Dead Sea has no outlet. The fresh water comes from the Jordan River and other tributaries, but it never leaves. As a result the water simply evaporates, leaving behind all the minerals in high concentration, which makes it impossible for plants, fish, or animals to populate the Dead Sea. No sea life can survive. In Ezekiel's vision, this miraculous river poured into this sea of death: "When it empties into the Sea, the water there becomes fresh" (Ezek. 47:8).

This river, which flowed from the temple, turned the Dead Sea into a living sea. "Swarms of living creatures will live wherever the river flows. There will be large numbers of fish, because this water flows there and makes the salt water fresh; so where the river flows everything will live" (Ezek. 47:9). The river is life-giving. Where it flows, everything will live. The prophet summarized the effects of this great river in words that reverberate through Scripture: "*Fruit trees* of *all kinds* will grow on both banks of the *river*. Their *leaves* will not wither, nor will their *fruit* fail. Every month they will bear, because the *water* from the sanctuary flows to them. Their fruit will serve for food and their leaves for *healing*" (Ezek. 47:12, italics added).

John the apostle, later the revelator, tells us that on the last and greatest day of the feast, or the seventh day, Jesus the Rabbi "stood and said in a loud voice . . ." (John 7:37). Rabbis customarily sat to teach. The word translated "loud voice" means literally to "scream." On the seventh day of the festival, after these passages had been read all week long, the ritual changed not in essence but in degree. Instead of going to the pool once, the priests went seven times, stoking the crowd's euphoria. Some commentators believe that it was after the water had been poured on the altar seven times and the priest had raised his hand to mark the end of the festival, that Jesus stood up and said in essence: "Now that I have your attention, I'd like to teach you something about the passages you've been reading all week!" (John 7:37, author's paraphrase).

The apostle John, who wrote this gospel account, also wrote the book of Revelation. He knew these passages of Scripture by heart, aware of the deep significance found in them for Christians. When we reach the end of the book of Revelation, John shares his sneak peak into heaven: "Then the angel showed me the *river* of the water of life, as clear as crystal, flowing from the throne of God and of the Lamb" (Rev. 22:1, italics added).

Here, John repeats a description of the river, a clear parallel to the earthly one—a revealing picture that proves the earthly river was a significant metaphor. The first difference found in John's description is that this river of life is flowing from the throne of Jesus, whereas the river of life in Ezekiel was flowing from the temple. John knew the connection between Jesus and the temple. In the second chapter of his gospel, he records a discussion between Jesus and His interrogators: "Jesus answered them, 'Destroy this temple, and I will raise it again in three days.' The Jews replied, 'It has taken forty-six years to build this temple, and you are going to raise it in three days?'" (John 2:19–20). Then John added an editorial comment for those reading his book: "But the temple he had spoken of was his body" (John 2:21).

In the Old Testament, the people came from near and far to the temple to connect with the one true, living God. Jesus on many occasions communicated that He was the new temple— through stories, arguments, activism (the turning over of tables in the temple), and the strange killing of a fig tree. No longer would people be forced to go to the temple to meet God. Now God had come to them in the person of Christ. So, in Ezekiel's vision, the water of life flowed from Christ; this was John's understanding of the water in Ezekiel too. Life always flows from Christ. He gives life to everything! Remembering the italicized words from Ezekiel, we see John showing us the connective tissue linking the Old Testament to the Messiah: ". . . down the middle of the great street of the city. On each side of the river stood the *tree of life*, bearing twelve crops of *fruit*, yielding its fruit every month. And the *leaves* of the tree are for the *healing* of the nations. No longer will there be any *curse*" (Rev. 22:2–3, italics added).

John added to the Ezekiel text: "no longer will there be any curse." When we read words like *tree of life* and *curse*, we are reminded of the creation account in Genesis: "The LORD God made all kinds of trees grow out of the ground—trees that were pleasing to the eye and good for food. In the middle of the garden were the *tree of life* and the tree of the knowledge of good and evil" (Gen. 2:9, italics added).

We remember the story. God gave man and woman a whole garden and only one restriction: Don't eat of the Tree of the Knowledge of Good and Evil. Eat of the Tree of Life, and live with Me forever in Paradise. Adam and Eve ate the forbidden fruit, and the results were, and have continued to be, catastrophic. One of the curses is recorded in Genesis 3:

> "The man has now become like one of us, knowing good and evil. He must not be allowed to reach out his hand and take also from the *tree of life* and eat, and live forever." So the LORD God banished him from the Garden of Eden to work the ground from which he had been taken. After he drove the man out, he placed on the east side of the Garden of Eden cherubim and a flaming sword flashing back and forth to guard the way to the tree of life. (verses 22–24, italics added)

So we lost access to the Tree of Life, and death became a stunning reality to mankind. The Tree of Life doesn't appear in Scripture again with a few exceptions in Proverbs, where it is used as a metaphor for wisdom. But then, like a lifebuoy bobbing up to the surface from man's wrecked ship, this passage appears in Revelation 22. In Eden, God said, "Here is my Tree of Life; eat it and live with Me forever." Then in heaven He will say again, "Here is my Tree of Life; live with Me forever."

But what about the *tweeners*, those born too late to live in

Eden, who haven't arrived in heaven yet? We discover the answer by returning to our Lord in the temple, standing and shouting: "If anyone is thirsty, let him come to *me* and drink. Whoever believes in me, as the Scripture has said, *streams of living water* will flow from within him" (John 7:37–38, italics added).

Here is that living river again, but this time Jesus said it will flow from within Him. The question scholars ask is: "What is the antecedent of *him?*" Who does the word *him* point to—Jesus or the person who comes to Jesus? Theologically I want to say Jesus, because we know all life flows from Him. Grammatically, many scholars agree that the phrase seems to point to the trusting person as the antecedent. This implies that the living water flows from the soul of the person who trusts in Christ.

Brilliant professors stand resolutely on both sides of the argument. This leads me to wonder if the ambiguity is intentional. Perhaps what Jesus is saying is that as the living water that originates in Jesus flows to receptive people, that living water then flows from the receptive people to touch the lives of other thirsty people. It would be nice to know exactly what this *living water* is. Fortunately, John added another editorial comment to clarify Jesus' words: "By this he meant the *Spirit*, whom those who believed in him were later to receive. Up to that time the Spirit had not been given, since Jesus had not yet been glorified" (John 7:39, italics added).

Jesus, at the time of speaking, hadn't yet been crucified, resurrected, or ascended to heaven, so the Spirit had not yet been sent to the disciples. But John clarified the imagery for us by defining the living water as the Holy Spirit of God. Knowing that the river of life is a symbol for the Holy Spirit allows us to understand all the river of life passages in that light.

Jeremiah was given the unenviable task of communicating to God's people that God's discipline was about to be enacted on them by the army of the Babylonians. Nothing in their power could stop it. Judgment was inevitable. He encouraged them to repent, not in order to beg God to relent from His plan, but so they could endure it in intimate fellowship with Him. God's sentence against them appears in Jeremiah:

> "Has a nation ever changed its gods? (Yet they are not gods at all.) But my people have exchanged their Glory for worthless idols. Be appalled at this, O heavens, and shudder with great horror," declares the LORD. "My people have committed two sins: They have forsaken me, the spring of living water, and have dug their own cisterns, broken cisterns that cannot hold water." (2:11–13)

They sinned by forsaking the one place they could find living water and by trying to create their own answers. A cistern was an underground holding tank where water was stored. God was telling them that their thirst for satisfaction was being quenched from leaky basins! David provides the contrast to this sin: "Oh God, you are my God, earnestly I seek you; my soul thirsts for you, my body longs for you, in a dry and weary land where there is no water" (Ps. 63:1).

David knew there was nothing but dry, arid desert outside the life-giving water of God. Gary Larson, of *The Far Side* fame, once drew a cartoon of two men dragging themselves through the dry desert in obvious agony from lack of water. They come across a functioning water fountain in the middle of a sand dune. As one of them pushes the button and bends down to drink, the other yells, "Wait until it gets cold!" When a body is thirsty to the point of dehydration, we don't wait around for the beverage to chill. We drink quickly and passionately.

David used the word *earnestly* to describe his longing for God. David knew that God was the only water fountain in the desert, the only place where his soul would find true satisfaction. Is it any wonder many Bible settings take place in the desert? After the eviction from Eden, God painted a picture of all of humanity wandering through life in the sand and heat. Jeremiah punctuated the story of man with the near-comical sketch of man finding his own cure for thirst with a leaky cistern. Our culture continues the search for satisfaction in material gain. The result is a culture of speed without rest and without trust. Like the leaky cisterns, Jeremiah contrasted these two types of people using the imagery we have gleaned from Scripture:

> This is what the LORD says: "Cursed is the one who trusts in man, who depends on flesh for his strength and whose heart turns away from the LORD. He will be like a bush in the wastelands; he will not see prosperity when it comes. He will dwell in the parched places of the desert, in a salt land where no one lives." (Jeremiah 17:5–6)

Like the contrast between Mary and Martha, the two sisters in the Gospels, we find ourselves in one of two places. This desert of frustration and stress called the modern life is the Martha place. The fundamental problem for Christians who are upset and worried is that like the children of Israel, they are trusting in themselves, depending on their own strength; or like Martha, they do not see the Savior sitting in their own living room. As a result, their hearts have turned away from the Lord, who is their strength. The result is a bleak picture of loneliness—dwelling . . . in a land where no one lives; fruitlessness—he will not see prosperity when it comes; and meaninglessness that relates to the wastelands (see Scripture above). There is a better place than the Martha place. The Mary place is described in Jeremiah 17:7–8:

> But blessed is the man who trusts in the LORD, whose confidence is in him. He will be like a tree planted by the *water* that sends out its roots by the stream. It does not fear when heat comes; its *leaves* are always green. It has no worries in a year of drought and never fails to *bear* fruit. (italics added)

David used almost identical terminology when he wrote of the blessed man: "He is like a tree planted by streams of water, which yields its fruit in season and whose leaf does not wither. Whatever he does prospers" (Ps. 1:3, italics added).

Jeremiah tells us that blessed people planted in the Holy Spirit have three distinguishing characteristics: they are courageous, healing, and fruitful.

Blessed People Are Courageous

At the beginning of the Operation Iraqi Freedom war, Americans ran out to hardware stores to buy duct tape and plastic sheeting to tape over household windows as a protection against potential chemical terrorist attacks. The major news publications ran stories about the fear that gripped our nation. The economy slumped, unemployment rose, and dangerous viruses such as AIDS spread at pandemic levels, leaving people frightened out of their wits.

During this new reign of fear, I was driving along the road with my eight-year-old son, Cameron, and asked him if he was scared of the terrorists. He said that he wasn't. So I asked him why he was not scared. He responded with resounding confidence, "Because we have the biggest army in the world, Dad!"

"Okay," I replied, and encouraged him to dig a little deeper.

He immediately jumped in, saying, "Because God loves us. Is that the answer you were looking for?" Like Cameron, we know the right answer, but it isn't always easy to live it. Fear can overtake our world and turn it upside down in the time it takes to allow the wrong person a seat on a plane.

A person rooted in the Spirit "does not fear when heat comes," and "has no worries in a year of drought." A person rooted in the Spirit does not fear terrorists, or bear markets, or unemployment, because their "confidence is in him" (see Jeremiah 17:7–8).

Keanu Reeves in the film *A Walk in the Clouds* was at odds with his fiancée's Old World family. In a drunken rage, the Spanish father and patriarch of the family's prestigious vineyard kicked over a lantern and set fire to the centuries-old estate. The lush vineyard was destroyed in one emotional act. But remembering the family's first ancestral vine, Reeves's character ran frantically to dig up the charred ancient plant. The grapevine's roots reached deep into the table water and fertile soil. Reeves sliced open the root to find that the plant was still green and alive. The vineyard was saved because of one root.

We live in an emotionally charged age. One altercation, one misplaced priority of one misguided soul, can rob us of our delicate balance. Where we plant our spiritual roots will determine our future latitude when crises and unexpected twists and turns mar our journeys. Roots are our silent life source, feeding our souls when we plant them deep in the spring of the Spirit.

Blessed People Provide Healing

People who place confidence in God also provide healing to those whose paths they cross during everyday life. Jeremiah said, "Its *leaves* are always green" (Jer. 17:8, italics added). Ezekiel emphasized, "Their fruit will serve for food and their leaves for *healing*" (Ezek. 47:12, italics added). John told us, "And the *leaves* of the tree are for the *healing* of the nations" (Rev. 22:2, italics added).

As a young boy, I created a terrarium of cacti, a living desert garden in my bedroom. An aloe vera plant centered the arrangement. One day while playing, I scraped my index finger. My friend took me to my room, broke off one of the stems from my aloe plant, and squeezed the fluid onto my scrape. The wound healed within two days.

The leaves of those who are planted in the Spirit bring healing to others in much the same way. The upset, worried, lonely, and dried-out person doesn't bring healing to others. Some who come in contact with hurting people—many times and without meaning to—inflict new wounds. Their own lives are as prickly and dry as a desert cactus. But a life broken open like the aloe vera leaf can bring incredible healing to a hurting world.

I received a late-night call a few years ago from one of our church families. Earlier that evening they had received a phone call informing them their twenty-year-old son had just died at college. They were devastated. I spent the evening exercising a ministry of presence as we sat around the room in shock. Some people, not knowing how to speak to a grieving person, may withdraw instead of just being a presence of love to that person. Those who exercise this ministry of presence during the early stages of shock will be remembered forever by the grieving as a healing balm.

A few weeks later, the mother of this boy came up to me at church and asked me if there was any ministry in our church that could aid her in her grieving process. I confessed there wasn't, but a local church in town had a grief ministry and I encouraged her to attend that group. She joined them, and after finding incredible healing and support, she started a grief group at our church. She has been broken, is planted in the river, and as a result, is energized to bring healing to a hurting world.

Blessed People Are Fruitful

My wife came home from the grocery store one weekend with nine different kinds of apples—I didn't know so many types existed. She washed them, cut them, and then placed them on numbered paper plates. We held a family apple-tasting contest—tasting each apple and then ranking them in order from one to nine. I liked the Pink Lady best. Like a SweetTart, it awakened the taste buds on both the front and back of my tongue. Fruit is a magnificent analogy of the impact the Holy Spirit has as He flows through us with His endless variety of uses, awakening our spirits to the varied nuances to which we can respond on so many spiritual planes.

John the Revelator said, "On each side of the river stood the *tree of life*, bearing twelve crops of *fruit*" (Rev. 22:2, italics added). It is peculiar to me that the tree of life is singular, but it is planted on both sides of a huge river. It comes to me that perhaps the tree of life is plural and singular at the same time. I think of the church as one body. Yet it is manifested in local bodies around the globe. In each local body are individual *trees* making up one *local tree*. This is the picture framed by Ezekiel: "When I arrived there, I saw a great number of trees on each side of the river" (47:7).

These trees, or people, produce fruit as the river gives them life. The fruit will vary because of our individual sphere of influence, giftedness, or season of life. But the fruit will be born, and the world will be touched.

> For true love is inexhaustible; the more you give, the more you have. And if you go to draw at the true fountainhead, the more water you draw, the more abundant is its flow.
>
> **—Antoine de Saint-Exupery**

So much rests on the river. The bush resides in parched land because it is far from the river. The tree brings healing and bears fruit in confidence, because it is rooted in the river. Here we find God's bottom line:

- From Jesus flows the Holy Spirit (John 16:7).

- From the Spirit flows life (Ezek. 47; Rev. 22; Ps.1).

- From life flows courage, healing, and fruit as the Spirit flows through us (Jer. 17).

When we personally and corporately remain rooted in the Spirit, we are the tree of life to a cursed world. The tree of life is the church of Jesus Christ, and those who make up that church. Christ sends the Spirit to us, the Spirit gives us life, and through us the Spirit brings healing and bears fruit. We root ourselves in the Spirit during times of sabbath rest so that He can be the fresh drink flowing into us. In the Great Shepherd

Psalm, David says to God: "The LORD is my Shepherd, I shall not be in want. He makes me lie down in green pastures, he leads me beside quiet waters, he restores my soul" (Ps. 23:1–3).

Libby and I recently spent a mini-sabbatical in the mountains of Colorado. After an intense time of ministry, we drove our rental car toward Estes Park and pulled into our bed-and-breakfast inn next to the Big Thompson River. Now the word *Big* in this title is relative in that it isn't Mississippi River big. But it apparently is bigger than the Little Thompson. We had left the children with my mom in Wisconsin, so we were able to truly rest. Reading Charles Dickens's *David Copperfield* by the side of the river for three or four hours at a time while one of our B&B mates pulled trout out of the frigid water on his fly rod was like heaven to me.

We also hiked up to the top of Twin Sisters Peak, walked through town, and ate at different restaurants. The river undulated throughout the mountain hamlet, omnipresent. The restaurants' conventions allowed us to dine near the river; the hikes we walked offered different views of the river; and the roads we drove tagged along after the river in a game of follow the leader. The river was a constant encouragement and delight to us, permeating our visit like fresh oxygen.

Libby also pointed out a strange observable fact. Some restaurants and places of business that possessed riverfront property failed to take advantage of its benefits. Instead of picture windows looking out over the Big Thompson, they had built their garages or parking lots facing the river, wasting the view.

Starved for beauty, we never devalued this life-giving waterway, but esteemed it highly. How much more likely are we, in our day-to-day affairs with business-as-usual, to build up our lives with our "garages" taking up the best views, while we press our noses to the back window glass, wishing for beauty and serenity? Our souls are restored beside the quiet brink at the river of Christ. He calls us down to the water, where we find complete and whole satisfaction. We shall not want. We are rooted in Him.

Secrets from the Wise Guys

6

Be silent in the presence of the Lord God; for the day of the Lord is at hand, for the Lord has prepared a sacrifice; He has invited His guests.

—ZEPHANIAH 1:7 NKJV

In his twenty-five-year career on the PGA Tour, Bruce Lietzke won thirteen events, which was a remarkable number of victories considering his limited play. Putting family first since 1989, Lietzke played in less than twenty events each year and yet remained competitive. With his children now grown, Lietzke, who turned fifty last July, joined the Senior PGA Tour and quickly won two events. Of the ten events he played, he had seven top-ten finishes. Off to a good start in 2002, he won the Audi Senior Classic in February and the TD Waterhouse in May.

Bruce is a bit of an anomaly on the tour. Back in the 1970s he was a rising star, winning tournaments and closing in on his first major title. Then his first child, a son, was born, and Bruce reduced his schedule, earning enough to live comfortably yet allowing him to stay at home and help with the rearing of his family. This lifestyle choice was not warmly received by many of his peers, some of whom complained that a younger player who desired to dedicate his life to golf could take Bruce's place on the tour. But Bruce's talent kept him in demand, allowing him to continue playing irregularly, winning enough events to stay on the tour.

In a recent conversation, Bruce told me, "In my early years on the PGA Tour, I thought it was important to play in every tournament I could so I could gain the experience and earn a living. Within two years I realized my best golf was played when I played three or four tournaments in a row, but my performance would always fall off if I continued to play consecutive events after those (initial) three or four."

Bruce was not physically tired after the third or fourth event, but he was mentally tired. He found a one- or two-week break after the third or fourth consecutive tournament would charge his batteries and bring back his enthusiasm. His consistency improved immediately.

Not long after this lesson came another one—playing the Pro-Ams or corporate outings on Mondays interfered with Bruce's handling of the letdown of tournament golf. Monday was a day to allow the adrenaline to leave his body and to begin the process of building up the adrenaline for another tournament. Monday golf outings did not allow Bruce time to relax and to prepare for the next tournament. Though the appearance money was good on Monday, his tournament paydays were suffering. Bruce stopped playing outings entirely; he was learning how to pace himself. Bruce Leitzke regulated his life around a healthy rhythm. Bruce discerned what a healthy rhythm looked like, and he stuck to it despite the opposition.

Like Bruce Leitzke, we are all given gifts that are handed to us through a genetic code at conception or through the heart of a teacher who fed us pearls instead of stones—gifts intended to be used as a means of glorifying God the Giver.

The world revels in its gifted, poking its straw into human lives to drink and taste of success, triumph, or artistry, sometimes taking until the person has nothing left to give. How often do we hear on the evening news of the gifted track star busted for steroid use or the famous actor arrested for illegal drug use, only to learn that an exploited life will not deliver a life of fulfillment?

To withdraw and give our bodies time to heal, our minds a day of relaxation, or our families an evening of cell phone–free, uninterrupted attention also ensures that we are guarding our gifts for a place of permanence in the lives of those we love most.

What does permanence look like? It is like the grain poured into the ground that sprouts to become the wheat that becomes the bread that feeds the hungry world. Permanence slips around the marketing whiz to confound the success gurus and disprove national statistics. Permanence is the daughter of wisdom, the offspring of long-suffering and waiting. She becomes the classic book, the perennial favorite. Permanence has a sense of the eternal and will be spoken from one generation to the next, always remembered, forever useful.

Stories birthed from a well-watered heart last and are passed along, perpetuated by those who recognize the value of wisdom and durability. The world can drink of it and grow strong and transformed instead of fat and greedy. The child can partake of it at his father's knee and know he is worth his father's time while the world is asked to wait to watch his daddy perform.

The ones who teach us the most about a time of stopping our work have also found a place of permanence. Joseph was more than a dreamer. He was a youth who found that, in the end, time off paid in high dividends.

Joseph's Involuntary Sabbatical

Joseph did not ask to be thrown into a cistern, sold into slavery, tricked into prison, and left to turn into cellar mold. But his brothers, full of bitterness and jealousy, forced him into a sabbatical that lasted throughout his coming-of-age years.

In modern society, we want our young people to perform like adults even before their minds have had a chance to mature and appreciate their own work. Young athletes are expected to rise at dawn and run until they are physically ill. Junior pianists are lauded as geniuses if they are performing on worldwide tours at the age of ten. The pressure to achieve is fed to modern children from the womb.

But we find Joseph as a young man rotting in a dingy stone dungeon, surrounded by the dregs of society, eating slop, waiting for vindication, and never seeing his court-appointed attorney. His future as a national leader remains shrouded in rejection, darkened by hopelessness. Yet his stellar attitude and favor with God never waned.

When interpreting the dreams of two cell mates one day— after a surrender to God for the answers—Joseph made one simple request: "When all goes well with you, remember me and show me kindness; mention me to Pharaoh and get me out of this prison" (Gen. 40:14). But when the cupbearer, in his jubilation to be free, forgot about him, Joseph sat waiting for two more years. The patience he exercised during this forced sabbatical strengthened his capacity to endure and ripened his maturity.

Note that Joseph did not attend leadership conferences. He did not spend his time cutting notches into his belt of achievement. We so often believe that by the spinning of our motivational wheels we are the sovereigns over our own achievements, when in reality we are the undeserved recipients of the Spirit's own breath upon our works.

After his rescue, ascension to power, and miraculous saving of the food sources of Egypt, he saw his brothers for the first time in years. When Joseph triumphantly revealed his identity to them—"So . . . it was not you who sent me here, but God" (Gen. 45:8)—he alluded to the fact that God had moved him into position geographically to arise as the famine buster he became.

Some like to argue that Joseph was young and arrogant but destined for greatness. God needed to prepare his heart and rout out the pride if he was to be useful in His master plan. I might agree, except I find no hint in the text that this was true. Instead, when he arrived in Egypt, he seemed to be completely enjoying God's favor, prospering and walking closely with God.

It seems we find no suggestion of pride in Joseph as he rebuffed the advances of Potiphar's wife. One might look long and hard for a reason for the two-year delay in the story, and never find one.

In his book *A Grace Disguised*, Gerald Sittser removed the temptation to quantify seasons of hardship in the chapter titled "The Terror of Randomness": "'Why did the tire blow out then and there?' we asked ourselves. We shivered with fear before the disorderliness of tragedy. If there was to be suffering, we at least wanted reason for it, predictability to it, and preparation to endure it. The randomness terrified us."[1]

As humans, we want to make algebra of our lives—to decipher the unknown variable and know that an answer follows the equation. God takes us through seasons marked by seemingly random variables—forced sabbaticals that leave us desperate and begging to never go through those places again. Yet at the end of them, we are somehow more usable to others who are stumbling around in the desert, thirsty and hungry. We do not find Joseph complaining, but somehow possessing an understanding that no matter what happened, God was God: "The LORD was with him . . . and granted him favor in the eyes of the prison warden" (Gen. 39:21).

Gerald Sittser experienced the worst season of hardship a man can face when he suddenly lost his wife, his daughter, and his mother. His brother-in-law, Jack, challenged Gerald to reconsider wanting the type of control that belongs solely to God. Sittser explained:

Did I really want to know what was going to happen in the future so that I could protect myself from the accidents that inevitably and randomly occur in every person's life? And if I knew what accidents were looming ahead and could change the course of my life, would I then want to know what accidents would befall me as a result of the new course I had set for myself? What I really wanted, he said, was to be God—an option obviously closed to me. So, if I really wanted to protect myself from accidents, he continued, I should lock myself inside an antiseptic bubble and live there for the rest of my life.[2]

Joseph trusted God in a way that not only allowed him to walk through a season of unexpected hardship, but eventually became part of a plan that would provide salvation for his family and an entire culture.

God values slowing down so much, He may choose to incarcerate us in an involuntary sabbatical for no obvious reason at all. I know about a man who suffers great emotional despair every time his company announces a series of layoffs, although he has yet to receive a pink slip. He fears a layoff to the point of physical illness, projecting what the sudden loss of a paycheck would mean to his family. Fear consumes him every autumn. As the leaves change color and fall from the southern foliage, he fears his life will fall away and turn to nothing.

Employers grant involuntary sabbaticals to their employees all the time. They pour themselves into the company for up to twenty years, showing loyalty and vigor along the way, only to show up one day and find their nameplates removed. They sit at home, working through the tension with their wives, the disappointment with the job search, and the plummeting self-esteem. The question always gets asked: Why? Why did this happen? Well there are obviously a lot of potential answers to that question: the sliding economy, poor job performance, unscrupulous bosses, and becoming too expensive on the raise chain all find their way onto the list. Sometimes, however, it isn't any of those things; it is simply God saying, "I want your attention for a while. I desire to be closer to you. I'm going to give you nine to ten hours a day off, just to sit, soak, be with Me, and recalibrate for the next lap."

My mom, Jill Briscoe, likes to say, "Don't waste your trials!" Joseph didn't.

Elijah's Emergency-Room Sabbatical

Ahab won the "worst king award" year after year when the votes were counted in heaven. He was described as doing "more evil in the eyes of the LORD than any of those before him" (1 Kings 16:30). He married Jezebel, that famous evil vamp who turned Ahab's heart toward the false god Baal and turned the nation of Israel into an idolatrous harlot. He provoked the Lord's anger, and God sent a messenger to confront him. The messenger's name was Elijah.

Elijah locked horns not only with Ahab and Jezebel but also with the 450 prophets of Baal in one of the great competitions recorded in the Bible. The end result was that Baal was proved to be a fraud, and the prophets of this false god were put to the sword by Elijah's command. (See 1 Kings 18.) This made him less than popular with the king's wife, who pledged to kill him by the next day. In a stunning response, Elijah got scared. He didn't back down from 450 men, but one woman had him running for the hills. (See 1 Kings 19:1–3.) He ran and hid, screaming out to God: "'I have had enough, LORD . . . Take my life.' . . . *Then he lay down under the tree and fell asleep*" (1 Kings 19:4–5, italics added)!

Prior to the "battle of the bulls," God gave Elijah a vacation. In 1 Kings 17 we see God lead Elijah to the Kerith Ravine so he could "drink from the brook" and be served hand and foot by flocks of ravens. It wasn't quite Club-Med. Elijah nevertheless took the free offer and rested. He drank, ate, and slept by the brook until the water dried up. At first, it seemed that Elijah accomplished nothing during this rest. However, as we continue on into the text, we realize that God's preparation of Elijah for a period of extreme ministry included a sabbatical of rest.

The physical and emotional output generated by the prophet of God as he stood on the mountain and took on the world is unimaginable. In facing Jezebel, the root of Elijah's anxiety was surfacing. Exhausted and at the end of his rope, he could no longer fight if God did not provide the prescriptive rest. Elijah might have faltered in the battle on Mount Carmel. A man crumbling in defeat halfway through the contest could not have glorified the Lord's name.

How many of us can recollect those times when opposition seemed to drop down on us like a jungle cat, and, because of our exhausted mental state, we succumbed to the attack? I remember such a day of testing in my own life.

My first day back from sabbatical was one of the hardest days of my ministry life. I went to an elders meeting that night excited to see my partners in ministry and geared to jump into the fall season with renewed energy. I was not prepared for what awaited me. One of the elders uncharacteristically and strongly confronted me. I was informed of areas of the church that were struggling, in terms that left me feeling defeated and angry. I left the meeting stunned and felt as though the entire reservoir of energy stored up during my time away had been depleted in one twenty-five-minute discussion.

Over the next few weeks, I worked through my anger with my friend and was able to separate the inappropriate communication style from the substance of the message. The fact remained that certain departments of our church had not kept up with our rapid growth. I commenced two and a half years of intense work with my team to fill the holes, and it was the most difficult period of my ministry. God knew in His infinite wisdom that this work lay ahead for me. As I was relaxing in His creation, He was replenishing me, preparing me for the extreme ministry that waited for me on my climb back up. Sometimes sabbaticals are taken for no apparent reason; others are needed to prepare for maximum outlay.

Only God knows what tomorrow brings. That is why we rest.

John's Working Sabbatical

My dad and I walked through the doors of our ship's cabin. I ducked my head as we passed through each door leading to the lobby of the cruise ship. We exited the gangplank and walked briskly over to the mules waiting nearby. We paid the fare and hopped onto the wooden saddles. The path up the side of the mountain weaved and wound past magnificent olive trees and around precipices that provided breathtaking views of the Mediterranean Sea. We arrived, sore-bottomed, at the little white-washed church building about two-thirds of the way to the summit of this soaring rock called Patmos.

As we walked into the chapel, my dad whispered to me, "Well, if you're going to be exiled, this isn't a bad place to be." He was speaking of the apostle John, the honorary namesake of the building in which we were now sitting. Our guide explained that this was most likely the very place that the beloved disciple of Jesus penned his apocalyptic masterpiece still preserved in our Bibles as the last book. John was on this splendid island "because of the word of God and the testimony of Jesus" (Rev. 1:9). On one Lord's Day during his sabbatical in paradise, the Spirit whisked John into a vision of heaven that he then dutifully recorded for generations of Christians. In this text we learn of the absolute certainty of the return of our Lord, the blessed hope that has for generations buoyed believers and motivated martyrs.

Most people are unaware that this wonderful work of God happened while John was on sabbatical. Granted, he would have preferred to be out planting churches and preaching the Word, but instead God placed him on an island in the middle of crystal aqua ecstasy. We cannot help but wonder if he felt guilty. John's sabbatical would be called a "working sabbatical," a phrase that sounds like an oxymoron.

But when John gave up his soul for God's service, his purpose took on a higher meaning. His life no longer his own, God's purpose replaced his human expectations of ministry. What may have seemed to John to be a benign pen-pal relationship with a few believers, God used to place a gargantuan punctuation point at the end of His legacy called the Holy Bible—a written work that turned the sticks of the apostle's journey into a spiritual bonfire.

A strange thing happens when we take some time to rest— God floods our minds with creative and Spirit-led ideas. My sabbatical journal is full of lessons I learned, struggles I confessed, relationships I want to mend, and books I want to write. It is truly remarkable how capable we are when we allow a little time for reflection.

Some sabbaticals may be classified as a study break. A week away for a mom to create a series of personal devotionals or for a pastor to develop a new preaching series is in fact a sabbatical. We can use the time to learn a second language or improve our health. Or, like John, we may find our lives suddenly secluded while God uses our small abilities to accomplish broader works in the masterpiece of His bigger picture.

However, the temptation to work through a sabbatical without rest follows the human mind like a fly to sugar. Prioritizing rest allows us to be a recipient of the Lord's ministry in our lives. We find joy in relaxing while we work on growth outside our daily responsibilities.

David's Sabbatical of Repentance

David took a sabbatical for the wrong reasons at the wrong time, and it led to all kinds of trouble. "In the spring, at the time when kings go off to war, David sent Joab out with the king's men" (2 Sam. 11:1), and he stayed behind to lounge on the roof. David should have been at work, but he chose to be at leisure instead. David's rhythm was out of whack. Unlike many of us, rest had superceded work.

We read that David rose from bed "in the evening." For too long, his eyes lingered over a beautiful woman, undressed and sunning on her roof. David, unable to take his thoughts off her, called for her to come to him, even though she belonged to another man. He slept with her, and she became pregnant. Desiring her for his wife, he manipulated circumstances to erase her husband from the scene, and they married, it seems, to live happily ever after. But then Nathan, the prophet of God, told David a touching story about a rich man stealing a poor man's only sheep.

David was infuriated until he realized the story was about him. His conscience guilt-stricken, he became inconsolable. He took another sabbath for the right reason at the right time. He retreated to his chambers and refused food. His infant son lay dying in the next room, a presumed judgment for his sin. We see David grieving, but not for the consequences of his sin; he is repulsed by the sin itself. We know this because it was at this time he wrote Psalm 51, the greatest confessional psalm in history. He admits his guilt; he pleads for mercy:

> Have mercy on me O God,
>   according to your unfailing love;
> according to your great compassion
>   blot out my transgressions.
> Wash away all my iniquity
>   and cleanse me from my sin . . .
> Surely I was sinful at birth,
>   sinful from the time my mother conceived me . . .
>   wash me, and I will be whiter than snow . . .
> Create in me a pure heart, O God,
>   and renew a steadfast spirit within me . . .
> Then I will teach transgressors your ways,
>   and sinners will turn back to you. (verses 1–2, 5, 7, 10, 13)

It was at this point that David put down his writing utensil and pulled out another piece of parchment. In his desire to teach transgressors how to turn back to God, he wrote Psalm 32, in which he trumpets the blessings of people who walk in repentance instead of walking in pretence:

> When I kept silent,
>   my bones wasted away
>   through my groaning all day long.

For day and night
   your hand was heavy upon me;
my strength was sapped
   as in the heat of summer.
Then I acknowledged my sin to you
   and did not cover up my iniquity.
I said, "I will confess
   my transgressions to the LORD"—
and you forgave the guilt of my sin. (verses 3–5)

David had been playing games with God, pretending that the sin had never occurred and presenting a persona of purity to the palace inhabitants. But inwardly he faced a spiritual death. The imagery is graphic. His strength was zapped from the inside out. Finally, he retreated to his chamber. In a confessional that became Psalm 51, he immediately sensed the guilt being lifted from him. David's latter sabbatical did not last long, but he found in it a precious purpose—to renew intimate fellowship between God and a wayward child.

We may need to take some time to reconnect with God through repentance and confession. The word *confess* in Psalm 32 means "to agree." God knows that we have sinned; we know that we have sinned. A person may read through the Psalm 32 passage above and sense the struggle resulting from a secret, sinful lifestyle. The description of burden and dry exhaustion hits close to home.

We can spend our time praying and reading through a sabbatical of repentance. We can name our sin to the Lord and renew our fellowship with Him. Then we can tell someone we trust. As long as it is a secret, it will control us. But as it is brought out into the open, in a manner of accountability, true healing can begin. As with Nathan, God in His infinite grace uses people close to us to bring us to a sabbatical of repentance.

My friend Dave had just returned from his father's funeral. He and his dad never really had a close relationship, and on careful examination, much of Dave's life had been spent attempting to gain his father's approval. With his dad now gone, much of what Dave had been living for was now gone too. Dave was extremely confused.

Gloria was one of the most beautiful women Dave had ever seen—and she was applying for a job in which she would report directly to him. Not only was she exceptionally attractive physically, but she was also bright, articulate, funny, engaging, and extremely charming—qualities necessary for the position. In fact, everyone in the organization who interviewed Gloria deemed her a "can't miss" prospect, and she was immediately hired.

For the first few weeks, things seemed innocent enough. While Dave (and every other man in his organization) found Gloria to be a head turner, he was more impressed by how quickly she caught on, how well clients responded to her, and what a great asset to the company she had become. Then one day, Gloria began to share with Dave a number of things that were going on in her personal life. She said that she appreciated that Dave seemed to be a man of integrity and that she felt close to God when she talked with him.

Over time, the intimate talks between Dave and Gloria became more frequent. The subjects they discussed became deeper and more personal until finally, Gloria shared with Dave how much she had grown to love him, and how attracted she was to him. "I feel like I have loved you for a thousand years," she said. "I know you are married, and I know I will never have *all* of you. But, I know I love you and I know I want to *make love* with you. Having only part of you is enough for me—I want you that much."

For a time, Dave resisted Gloria admirably. He prayed like crazy. He asked God for help. He tried to "take every thought captive" and struggled to fight off the temptation in his mind. He even shared the gospel with her. However, deep down inside, Dave really *wanted* Gloria, and it was intoxicating for him to be wanted *by* her. He tells of hearing things in his thought life like: "This is a gift from your Father (dad) in heaven."

Not knowing this was stuff from Satan himself, Dave began to actually *believe* it. He also heard: "Go for it. You *deserve* it. God knows that your wife will never meet *all* your needs, and of all the men in the world, Gloria wants you! Take it while you can get it! It's okay." So, like a sheep led to slaughter, Dave succumbed to the temptation—led by his own evil desires—and entered into an extramarital affair with Gloria.

For a while, it was actually fun for Dave—like a big game. But the more involved he became with Gloria, the more strange things became in his world. He lost his voice. He grew extremely sick. Ants infested his house. What his son's preschool teacher called "devils," tormented his toddler son. Things began to go sour at his job. His behavior became irritable and erratic. He was completely self-absorbed. When first confronted about his strange behavior, Dave lied to everyone he knew. He lied to his wife. He lied to his friends. He lied to his pastor, and he lied to God. Then one rainy night Dave's wife looked him in the eye and asked him, "Are you having an affair with Gloria?"

Faced for the first time with the severity of his sin, and overcome with guilt, grief, and despair, Dave replied, "Now I know what the Bible means when it says, 'Sin is death.'" Even though he confessed his sin and knew what he was doing was wrong, Dave surprisingly chose to stay in the affair. A few days later, he separated from his wife. Shortly after that, he lost his job.

While Dave prayed blindly for God's guidance and direction throughout this ordeal, he had convinced himself that leaving his wife and son was "the right thing to do." Then, his pastor (and best friend at the time) confronted him "man to man." He said, "Dave, I love you. Your wife loves you. Your son loves you, and I know that God loves you. But you are in a wicked delusion. You've been deceived by Satan, and I'm telling you right now that you are walking down the road to destruction. All I can say is that I would *like* to be here for you, but I *can't* be here for you. If you're going to continue this life of sin, I must get out of the picture—because I want nothing to do with it. Now, I'll be here if you make the right choices, but until you do, I'm out of here. I hate that this is the way it has to be, but this is the way it has to be. Good-bye."

With that said, his pastor left the scene. Dave had never felt more alone in his life. Out of work and seemingly out of hope, Dave decided that he needed to prepare his house for sale. A section of his yard needed a lot of work, so Dave decided that he would try to clean it up by himself. As he worked his land and began to dig up the weeds, Dave cried out to God, and God began to clearly speak to his heart: "*I'm* the Father for whom you should be living. I *love* you. I have *always* loved you. *I* gave you your wife, and *she* loves you. Your *son* loves you. *Follow Me, and I will make your path straight.*"

Overwhelmed at God's gentle yet direct nudging, Dave fell to his knees, cried like a baby, repented of his sins, and began the long and arduous process of putting his life (and the life of his family) back together. Dave and his wife reconciled, and God blessed them richly. Their son has grown to be a solid, godly young man, and they now have a beautiful young daughter, who gave her life to Christ at an early age. Their key ministry? Coming alongside couples who are in the midst of marital crisis.

God shows us that He is still in control even when we run the wrong way. He pays attention to all of our wanderings with His telescopic heart. When we stop and grow quiet, He speaks to us, as He did to Dave, from the weed patches of our lives. Reaching in past the briars and nettles, God fashions the weeds of our past for another use, as men shaped crowns from the thorn bed for a sovereign's brow. He risks the scratches and wounds of our sin to reach in and get to us. That is how badly He desires to draw us close to Himself.

Paul's About-Face Sabbatical

"I will not yield my glory to another," God tells us through the prophet (Isa. 48:11). He often puts people to work in areas outside their expertise. When He operates through us yet outside of our abilities, then God takes proper credit. We find this practice repeated by God in many examples from numerous unlikely Old and New Testament heroes:

- *David* was a shepherd, and God made him a king.
- *Deborah* was a housewife, and God made her a leader.
- *Rahab* was a prostitute, and God made her a deliverer.
- *Peter* was a fisherman, and God made him a churchman.
- *Matthew* was a tax collector, and God made him an author.
- *Luke* was a doctor, and God made him a historian.
- *Mary Magdalene* was demon-possessed, and God made her a benefactor.

And in church history:

- *Martin Luther* was a Catholic priest, and God made him a Reformer.
- *Billy Graham, Bill Bright, Major Ian Thomas,* and *Dawson Trotman* all rose from humble beginnings to make an amazing impact on the world for Christ. Each life passed credit back to the One who deserved the recognition.
- The greatest example in history of this "about-face" theory of assignment is the *apostle Paul*. In the melee of his arrest in Jerusalem, Paul asked for permission to address the Jewish crowd: "I am a Jew, born in Tarsus of Cilicia, but brought up in this city. Under Gamaliel I was thoroughly trained in the law of our fathers and was just as zealous for God as any of you are today" (Acts 22:3).

In other words, Saul was an "all-pro Jew" at the top of his religious game. Raised in the city of the Jews, trained under the premier rabbi of the day, and climbing the corporate menorah, he was the rising star of all things Jewish. But God sent him to the Gentiles, an act that would be on par with asking Shaquille O'Neal to become a jockey.

In his personal testimony about the amazing day Jesus appeared to him on the road to Damascus, Paul recounted his marching orders: "Then the Lord said to me, 'Go; I will send you far away to the Gentiles'" (Acts 22:21).

God needs no strategic planner to help Him with His plan of attack. Why wouldn't God send Paul to the Jews? By sending the "wrong" person to the Gentiles, God knew the glory for Paul's work would find its way to Him. So he sent a poor public speaker, one who was an expert on Jewish law and history, to the world of the Gentiles to preach the gospel. After his conversion, Paul immediately started to preach in Damascus. Then the Lord took him away for a rest. Paul described the sabbath this way:

> I was advancing in Judaism beyond many Jews of my own age and was extremely zealous for the traditions of my fathers. But when God, who set me apart from birth and called me by his grace, was pleased to reveal his Son in me so that I might preach him among the Gentiles, I did not consult any man, nor did I go up to Jerusalem to see those who were apostles before I was, but I went immediately into Arabia and later returned to Damascus. (Galatians 1:14–17)

Superstars strive for approbation; heroes walk alone. Superstars crave consensus; heroes define themselves by the judgment of a future they see it as their task to bring about. Superstars seek success as a technique for eliciting support; heroes pursue success as the outgrowth of inner values.

—**Henry Kissinger**

Paul had received a commission outside his expertise. In this text again we see his precipitous rise in Judaism juxtaposed with his call to the Gentiles. How will he prepare himself for his task? Will he go to a seminar or set up appointments for individual meetings with self-proclaimed gurus on Gentile behavior? No, he exclaims, *I did not consult any man!* Instead, he went to Arabia, a vast territory. We are not given exactly where Paul went in Arabia. But we do know he went by himself for a period of time and allowed God to prepare him for his new task.

After returning to Damascus, visiting Jerusalem, and initiating his mission, the Jews revolted against him. For his own protection the other disciples "took him down to Caesarea and sent him off to Tarsus" (Acts 9:30). Most commentators believed he remained for seven or eight years—an elongated sabbatical before the first of his three great missionary journeys. Even though he was a Jew of Jews, Paul's effectiveness congealed in his mission to the Gentiles because he allowed God to mold him in times of studious quiet when he was alone and away.

We go through periods where we sense a change coming into our lives, but we cannot see over the precipice of our current situations to find the next turn in the road. A time of sabbath rest allows us to hear God's call clearly and prepares our hearts for the new assignment. We have to remember that God usually calls with a double leading. God doesn't call us to a new situation without calling us from the old one.

A man may "feel called" to leave his position at work or in a ministry—especially after a poor performance review, declining attendance, or a salary cut—yet have no opportunities into which he may move. Conversely, a pastor or business manager may *sense* God's direction to accept a more attractive job package, even though there is no indication that her present work is completed.

By taking time away to look for God's clear direction, we can hear His evaluation of the situation.

In Billy Graham's autobiography, we are introduced to a farm boy from Park Road outside Charlotte, North Carolina. Now bearing a household name, Graham has helped millions of lives to follow Christ.

In the early years, Chuck Templeton had left the pastorate in Toronto to enroll at Princeton Theological Seminary. While there he struggled with theological issues surrounding the authority of Scripture and eventually challenged Graham on his commitment to Scripture. "Billy, you're fifty years out of date. People no longer accept the Bible as inspired the way you do. Your faith is too simple, your language is out of date, and you're going to have to learn new jargon if you're going to be successful in your ministry."[3]

Graham's resolve started to crumble under the weighty influence of Templeton. Maybe he was too simple, he thought. He wasn't nearly as brilliant as Templeton, and only a farm boy. With the Los Angeles crusade looming on the horizon, Graham went on a retreat to the mountains of California. He poured his heart out to Henrietta Mears, who was at this time the director of religious education at First Presbyterian Church of Hollywood, and the head of the conference that week. Mears confirmed her strong belief in the authenticity and veracity of Scripture. In turmoil, he sat in his room alone and read every passage he could find that used the words "thus saith the Lord." He prayed, and the thought came to him: *I'm only thirty years of age. It's not too late to be a dairy farmer.* He left his room and in the moonlight walked in the woods of the San Bernardino Mountains.

> Dropping to my knees there in the woods, I opened my Bible at random on a tree stump in front of me . . . The exact wording of my prayer is beyond recall, but it must have echoed my thoughts, "O God! There are many things in this book I do not understand. There are many problems with it for which I have no solution . . ." I was trying to be on the level with God, but something remained unspoken. At last the Holy Spirit freed me to say it. "Father, I am going to accept this as Thy Word—by

faith!" . . . In my heart and mind, I knew a spiritual battle in my soul had been fought and won.[4]

Graham went on to Los Angeles with the freedom to be a farm boy from North Carolina with a calling to tell the world the good news.

We question God perhaps at times unceasingly. He houses His Spirit within the architecture of our own hearts and sends out minute-by-minute invitations to enter, so that in the quiet of an afternoon or on a moonlight stroll, we can hear. It is an unlocked door that only requires us to reach for its handle.

Jesus' Sabbaticals

Jesus had numerous sabbaticals. He went away to be reenergized through prayer, quiet meditation, and to spend personal time with close friends. Jesus spent forty days alone in the wilderness prior to His ministry, but we should remember that He went into the wilderness on that occasion specifically to be tempted by the evil one (see Matthew 4:1).

Jesus, like many of us, was either unable or unwilling to spend large amounts of time away from His responsibilities. So He maintained a wise rhythm in the midst of His ministry life. In addition to His custom of taking the weekly Sabbath—"He went to Nazareth, where he had been brought up, and on the Sabbath day he went into the synagogue, as was his custom" (Luke 4:16)— Jesus incorporated other forms of time off into His life.

We see evidence of time off after a period of victory. After the miraculous feeding of the five thousand, "immediately Jesus made the disciples get into the boat and go on ahead of him to the other side, while he dismissed the crowd. After he had dismissed them, he went up on a mountainside by himself to pray. When evening came, he was there alone" (Matt. 14:22–23).

Jesus would most likely have agreed with the sign on a wall of the visitor center at the Air Force Academy in Colorado Springs:

"The will to win means nothing unless you have the will to prepare." But He would also have argued that time away after great ministry is imperative. Could it be, with His commitment to humility, Jesus got away to connect with the Father in an attempt to stay grounded and to fight off pride?

We see Jesus taking time off before making major decisions. "One of those days Jesus went out to a mountainside to pray, and spent the night praying to God. When morning came, he called his disciples to him and chose twelve of them, whom he also designated apostles" (Luke 6:12–13). The choice of the disciples was most likely not an easy task. Jesus had a fairly substantial group following Him around at this point. But He knew He needed to choose the leaders that would take His good news to the nations. Before making the decision, He prayed all night long.

He also took time off after a heavy period of ministry. "The apostles gathered around Jesus and reported to him all they had done and taught. Then, because so many people were coming and going that they did not even have a chance to eat, he said to them, 'Come with me by yourselves to a quiet place and get some rest.' So they went away by themselves in a boat to a solitary place" (Mark 6:30–32).

A few years back I started to "get some rest" too on the Monday after each Easter. Although we offered four service times on Sunday morning, we added one more for Easter Sunday. After preaching at five services one Easter, I went back to the office the next day and a few hours later crumpled to the ground with back spasms. Fatigued by the emotional and physical outlay of the Good Friday and Easter weekend services, my body demanded rest. By prioritizing a sabbath on my calendar before Great Week comes, I have been able to maintain emotional health and keep my back from giving out.

Jesus took time off when He'd had enough of people. "Jesus left that place and went to the vicinity of Tyre. He entered a house and *did not want anyone to know it;* yet he could not keep his presence secret" (Mark 7:24, italics added).

Jesus wearied of constant people-contact just as we do. Even those of us who are off-the-chart extroverts have our people limits. So He hid away at a friend's house in hopes of finding seclusion. Even the disciples were ignorant of His plans. He needed a rest from them too. By taking a people break, we give our bodies time to refuel so that when our lives integrate once more with others', what comes out of us will be sincere and productive. Of course, Jesus' hideout was quickly discovered, and He did serve the needs of those who tracked Him down. Life doesn't always follow a tidy schedule. In planning spur-of-the-moment time off, we have to prepare for flexibility. But when we feel the pressure cooker of people draining us of all energy, we can remember that even Jesus took time away.

Jesus also took time off when He faced an intimidating task. When He arrived on the Mount of Olives the night of His betrayal, "He withdrew about a stone's throw beyond them, knelt down and prayed" (Luke 22:41). The content of His prayer was, in essence: "Dad, do You have a plan B, and can we discuss it now?" Jesus was human—terrified of the Cross, the pain, and the humiliation—but He knew He had to do it. So what did He do? He went off alone to pray.

In this brief survey of biblical heroes, we have seen sabbaticals of varied duration: two years, "a short time," the remainder of a life, long enough to write two psalms, seven years, overnight, and a single evening.

As demonstrated by our heroes, other reasons for a sabbatical are fear, exhaustion, being "peopled out," preparation, humbling oneself, to recalibrate for a different kind of ministry, repentance, productivity, and, in Joseph's case, no obvious reason at all. The form, duration, reasons for, and activities of sabbaticals may vary greatly. All these heroes of faith from Scripture participated in some form of rest. The people in the Bible that made a difference, made a practice of taking a sabbath rest. For some, God had to force it upon them. Others volunteered, but they all faced a period of rest at some time. We, being of the same ilk and fallible nature, must fall in line behind the wise guys.

Bruce Lietzko and I played a round of golf one afternoon. His advice to me was to always play with the swing with which I was most comfortable. I noticed that he always hit the ball from left to right. This is called a fade. I hit my ball right to left, a shot called a draw. After Bruce advised me how to swing, I applied his advice and focused on simply hitting the ball with a draw every time. When we got to the seventh hole, Bruce found himself flush up against the left side of the fairway, with large trees making a fade shot impossible. I wondered what he would do. Standing over the ball, he took a mighty swing and hit a magnificent *draw* onto the green, instead of his usual fade. I stood dumbfounded. "Didn't you say we should always play what we are comfortable with? You just hit a draw!"

He smiled and said, "Pete, I'm a professional. I've got all the shots."

This fact was dramatized recently. In 2003, Bruce, now playing sporadically on the Senior's Tour, was leading the Senior U.S. Open in the third of four rounds. Johnny Miller, the commentator and himself a former great player, was subtly criticizing Bruce for wasting his talent with the lifestyle decisions he had made. Eventually, he intimated that Bruce wouldn't have the mental toughness to win a major. In the final round, Bruce found himself in an almost impossible place on the golf course after an errant tee shot. The only possible way to hit the green was to play a huge draw, which Miller didn't even consider an option. Bruce stood over the ball and hit a magnificent draw just short of the green, putted for his par, and went on to win the tournament. Miller was speechless—a rare spectacle.

Bruce can play all the shots, but he has made a choice to play the fade most of the time. This is because he knows he will be most successful if he does so. But he also realizes that sometimes we have to break the mold and be flexible. Bruce could have run the race among the fast and furious, made tons of money, and etched his name in golf lore. But he chose a different road.

As he stood on the eighteenth green accepting the Senior U.S. Open trophy, the interviewer said to Bruce, "You realize that winning this tournament wins you the right to play in the U.S. Open on the regular tour next year. What do you think about that?"

Bruce responded, "I'm sorry I can't make it. My family has a weekend at the lake house planned."

Life's treadmill sets the pace for us only if we let it. Wise guys finish happy.

The Rest of the Gospel

> These things I have spoken to you, that in Me you may have peace. In the world you will have tribulation; but be of good cheer, I have overcome the world.
>
> —JOHN 16:33 NKJV

At Christmastime the familiar refrain of Isaiah 9:6 echoes through the sanctuaries of local churches:

> For to us a child is born, to us a son is given, and the government will be on his shoulders. And he will be called Wonderful Counselor, Mighty God, Everlasting Father, Prince of Peace.

The Prince of Peace is an ideal nomenclature, considering our need for a sabbath rest. Jesus, no ordinary prince, came to Earth all but camouflaged. No trumpets at the palace gates heralded His arrival. In fact, He came unexpectedly like no other prince from this planet.

He came dressed as a blue-collar worker. In fact, the book of Isaiah spells out the sobering fact that He was nothing special to look at. Actually, Jesus was most likely (considering the average man of His day) about five feet tall, frequently unbathed, unshaven, and unkempt. He most likely struggled with His eyesight, perhaps could not have gotten a brush through His matted hair, and had lost most of His teeth by the date of His crucifixion. He was, in reality, the antithesis of the pristine, handsome depictions we now see in the framed art sections of Christian bookstores.

G. K. Chesterton wrote of Christ:

> There I found an account, not in the least of a person with His hair parted in the middle or His hands clasped in appeal, but of an extraordinary being with lips of thunder and acts of lurid decision, flinging down tables, casting out devils, passing with the wild scenery of the wind from mountain isolation to a sort of dreadful demagogy; a being who acted like an angry god—and always like a god.[1]

He arrived as a nomad of the desert. Jesus had no place to rest His head (see Matthew 8:20). If Jesus walked our earth today, we would be more likely to find Him under a bridge, a vagrant homeless man, than in a suburban home. Prince of Peace?

Jesus, much to the chagrin of His disciples, did not enter the world to run for office (or to run off the present officers, which was the way power was wielded in those days). He came to birth peace, not to wage war, but He did not rush into explanations. Yet through His life He redefined faith. He taught and modeled the ridiculous concept of turning the other cheek—taking blows instead of leveling His opponents.

Then one day, after the baby born that winter night had grown into a man, He described how the peace He brought to Earth could actually be found. At last He was offering the new definition: "Come to me, all you who are weary and burdened, and I will give you rest. Take my yoke upon you and learn from me, for I am gentle and humble in heart, and you will find rest for your souls. For my yoke is easy and my burden is light" (Matt. 11:28–30).

"Rest for your souls." So much of the unrest in our lives stems from a misunderstanding of the basic components of the gospel. Most of us in evangelical circles understand the first part: "Come to me . . . and I will give you rest," but we experience a disconnection with the second half of the text—"Take my yoke upon you." To state the overarching principle of this Scripture, we must understand that if we want to find rest in our souls, we need to grasp the rest of the gospel.

The First Part of the Gospel

"I specialize in pain," said the small Hispanic man standing between my office and me. He had walked in as my savior. I had just finished preaching my fourth morning service and was in agony. My injured back was in a spasm, making it impossible to stand up straight. I looked like a human question mark. I had to sit down to preach the last service because the pain had weakened my legs. Ed approached me after the service, wanting to help me with my dilemma. He specialized in pain?

"Giving it or relieving it?" I asked.

"Yes," came the reply. "I'll be at your house at two this afternoon. I'll get you back on your feet."

Ed showed up as promised. I limped to his traveling massage table and lay facedown. He took his vise-grip hands, searched for the knots in my back, and proceeded to knead them out. For two and a half hours, he wrestled with my pain—pushing, prodding, poking, and driving the spasm away, every motion a momentary pain that spiked and then subsided. When I eased off the table I could stand up straight.

"I'll see you again tomorrow," he told me, "and the next day. Then I want to see you once a week to keep you in shape." He smiled as he headed out the door. The thought came to me: *Maybe I won't have to live in pain anymore.*

For two years Ed kept my back straight, volunteering his time, energy, and expertise to bear my pain with me. While I lay on that table we talked. He opened up and shared candidly with me some of the hardships he had overcome. We prayed together. But when he told me one day that the doctors had found a tumor in his head, my heart almost stopped. The cancer spread rapidly. Soon Ed was unable to work on my back. Then he lost his ability to walk. I sat by his sickbed with his precious wife, trying to somehow reciprocate the support he had shown me.

Small to begin with, Ed almost shriveled from sight before our eyes. Bad back and all, I picked him up one day to adjust the bedsheets. I watched the smiling eyes slowly lose their light. His face had aged almost day by day, his skin turning into loose folds. Then one morning as the sun rose, Ed died. I mourned his loss; not because I no longer had a gifted masseur at my disposal, but because through his compassion, friendship had formed between us. Now my friend was gone. But before he left me, he touched me in a way that made my journey lighter.

When someone notices our suffering and offers to help us selflessly, it is like offering to carry our backpack after we've sojourned a hundred friendless miles. Even though it has been six years since Ed died, you will often hear in our house the words "I miss Ed," because we dearly do.

Jesus walked the earth, a careful observer, noticing our suffering and then offering permanent relief.

"Come to me, all you who are weary and burdened, and I will give you rest."

Walt Wangerin enriched Christian literature with a story of how his father administered calamine lotion to his "dreadful case of poison ivy," an irritation made worse by his mother's application of soap:

> I knew that calamine lotion was utterly useless even if it could get to the rash; but *my* rash was covered by a rind of Fels Naptha soap. No good. No good.
>
> Nevertheless, when my father appeared again with a giant bottle of the stuff; when my father knelt down beside the bed, uncovered me, and began so gently with his own hand to rub it on; when my father's eyes damped with the tears of suffering, so

that I saw with wonder that my pain had actually become his own pain and that it was our pain that had sent him rocketing to the drug store; when I saw and felt that miracle, a second miracle took place: the ivy did not itch.

Calamine lotion did not do this thing!

My father's love did this thing—and I knew it! Oh, my heart ached to have such a father, who could enter into me and hurt so much that he took my hurt away.[2]

Jesus sends a blanket invitation to everyone who is "tired of trying" and "tired of carrying" to come to Him for relief. In Matthew 11, the word translated *weary*, is active, describing those who have become tired through heavy struggle. Jesus was alluding to those who have invested all their energy trying to earn God's favor, finding themselves exhausted and discouraged.

The word *burdened*, the passive side of weariness, sketches a picture of overloaded beasts of burden, groaning under the weight of the master's expectations. Humans struggle under a modern yoke of oppression and unbalanced loads.

Many words in the English language originated with a rudimentary semantic range, only to develop into deep, rich words. When the Hebrew word for *yoke* appeared on the scene, it was a farming word describing the wooden instrument strapped across two beasts of burden to facilitate the sharing of heavy loads. In time it came to mean a myriad of things that can be grouped together and summarized in two categories: either something shared or something placed upon you.

The idea of something shared follows naturally from the original meaning of the word. By hooking into the heavy piece of wood, the two animals are able to partner in the work, thus making it easier, more pleasant, efficient, and successful. Extrabiblical Jewish literature saw wisdom as a yoke, the ability to share life's struggles together.

The Bible echoes this sentiment in Lamentations 3:27. Jeremiah said: "It is good for a man that he bear the yoke in his youth" (KJV), speaking of the law and wisdom. In Jeremiah 5:5, the notion of this yoke of wisdom is applied to knowing God's way and expectations: "'So I will go to the leaders and speak to them; surely they know the way of the LORD, the requirements of their God.' But with one accord they too had broken off the yoke and torn off the bonds.'"

Wisdom, the law, God's way, and His expectations were all shared as a way to make life easier, more pleasant, efficient, and successful. When a yoke is shared, it is a positive addition to your life. A partnership.

When a yoke is thrown upon us, however, it is oppressive and leads to exhaustion and frustration. This theme is demonstrated throughout the Old Testament. In Exodus 6, it is the yoke of Egyptian slavery, in Isaiah 14 we read of the yoke of Assyrian oppression, and in Isaiah 47 the Babylonian yoke weighs heavily on the people of Israel. In Jeremiah 27, Jeremiah wore a yoke around his neck as a symbolic sermon of the coming oppression of the Babylonians.

When a yoke was placed upon a nation or an individual, the weight was too much to bear. This is exactly what the pharisaical leaders of Jesus' day had done to the masses. They had taken the yoke of the law and thrown it on the necks of the people, adding weight with additional rules and regulations. Matthew offers a blatant example as the Pharisees condemn Jesus and His disciples for picking grain and healing the sick on the Sabbath. When we read Matthew 23:1–4, we can almost picture these pious frauds throwing the wooden beams over the hunched shoulders of the people of God:

> Then Jesus said to the crowds and to his disciples: "The teachers of the law and the Pharisees sit in Moses' seat. So you must obey them and do everything they tell you. But do not do what they do, for they do not practice what they preach. [In other words, they do not share this yoke with you.] They tie up heavy loads [this is the same word translated as *burdens* in Matthew 11] and

put them on men's shoulders, but they themselves are not willing to lift a finger to move them."

So Jesus looked at the masses, those weary from trying to follow all the rules, those burdened by the weight of the pharisaical yoke, and laid out the massage table while He said simply, "Come to me." *Come to Me—I Am will* give *you rest.*

Soul peace is a gift from the Prince. Jesus lovingly says, "I am a different kind of prince. I am not endorsing a new set of regulations; I am inviting you to a new kind of relationship. Not a fidelity to a code, but a dedication to a person." *Come to Me, and I will* give *you rest.* Soul rest is not earned but received. Salvation is not adherence to rules and regulations; it is simply coming to the One who fulfilled all the rules and regulations and standing with Him.

When I taught these principles in my church in Dallas, two people came up onto the stage and placed a real wooden yoke over the neck of one while I explained how oppressive it is when a yoke is placed upon us. The effect of the yoke was apparent: his knees crumpled, his face turned red, he quickly became weary and burdened, and I kept teaching. Then I had the other man come alongside and carry the yoke with him, and we saw a picture of the *rest* of the gospel.

The Rest of the Gospel

Sharing a yoke is unlike a three-legged race. I remember those relays at family picnics or youth camp, the awkwardness, the discomfort, and the deep desire to be free of the awkward ten-year-old strapped to my calf. Sharing a yoke is not an added burden, but a burden relieved. It is a friend helping you move your piano, a sister listening to your story, a small-group member bringing you dinner; it is the Lord walking with you through life. Jesus employs the imagery of the yoke and reverts to the original meaning of the word to paint a picture of the Christian life:

"Take my yoke upon you." Jesus is not offering the yoke of the

law, neither is He offering a life free from constraints. Jesus is offering to share life with us, thus making it easier, more pleasant, efficient, and successful. When Jesus uses the word *yoke*, it is a metaphor for *discipleship*, you voluntarily strapping yourself to Him.

"*. . . and learn from me.*" The word *learn* is *mathete*, taken from the root word *manthano*, which means "to learn from experience." One derivation of this word is *mathates*, translated as *disciple* in our English Bibles.

In the fields, when smart farmers coupled a wild ox with a well-tamed ox, the wild one, confined, constrained, and trained, became tame too. When Jesus says, "Come to Me," this is the life to which He is calling us. We are the wild ones, yoked to the perfect One, confined, constrained, and trained to live this abundant life, to find rest. Jesus promises this calming of the soul to those who volunteer for the yoking.

"*For I am gentle and humble in heart, and you will find rest for your souls.*" This is a direct quote from Jeremiah 6:16: "This is what the LORD says: 'Stand at the crossroads and look; ask for the ancient paths, ask where the good way is, and walk in it, *and you will find rest for your souls*'" (italics added). The good way, the ancient way is fulfilled in Jesus. Walking with Him is where rest is found. And you will *find* rest. It simply happens, as we walk in a close, intimate gait with Jesus. Our weariness leaves, our burden is lifted, and rest creeps into our souls.

"*For my yoke is easy and my burden is light.*" *Easy* probably isn't the best translation of the original word *chrestos*. Other translations include "kindly," "good," "comfortable," and "well-fitting." The life of discipleship isn't necessarily easy, but being yoked to Jesus makes the difficult aspects of life easier than they would be if walking alone through pain.

When He says the burden He carries with us is *light*, He is reminding us that He calls us not to oppressive, external commands, but instead to loyalty to a person. Here is the offer Jesus makes: You can live the rest of your life under the burden of the law, rules, trying and hoping, or you can come to Me, receive My gift, align yourself with Me and learn. In the process of that discipleship relationship, you will find rest for your soul.

What does God want me to think, know, feel, or do? What does this incredible passage mean for me today?

Receive the gift of *rest* from the Prince of Peace.

Embrace the *rest* of the gospel.

Stop placing yokes on the necks of others.

Tell the rest of the world the rest of the gospel.

Receive the Gift of *Rest* from the Prince of Peace

This is obviously the first step. Those who are tired of trying and exhausted from carrying may receive the free gift of salvation and rest that Jesus offers. The Bible teaches that our sin has separated us from God, but Jesus, who is fully God, became fully man to die and shed His blood for us. It was necessary for blood to be shed because life is found in blood. Anyone who comes to the cross of the perfect One who sacrificed Himself for us will have his or her sins erased and will be declared righteous before God. That's what Jesus means by "Come to Me."

Embrace the *Rest* of the Gospel

One of the unfortunate and unintentional ramifications of the revivalist movements of previous centuries is the notion that Jesus is quite happy to simply save us and then let us go our own way. Nothing could be farther from the truth. Jesus saves us to yoke us. Jesus said, "Come to Me—My yoke."

Why is it that American nonbelievers' lifestyles so closely resemble believers' lifestyles? Why are divorce and pornography statistics the same regardless of church affiliation? Gossip runs rampant; materialism goes unchecked in both communities. I am convinced that many people in churches have heeded the "come to me" portion of the text, but have neglected the yoke. We are all excited about the free gift of salvation, but we neglect the fact that this free gift costs us everything. We are thrilled to be Christians, but we reject the call to be disciples. Thus there is little or no change in our lives. Instead of rest, chaos, war, and weariness rule our souls. By taking our walks with Jesus seriously, our peace in Jesus can impact us tremendously.

Stop Placing Yokes on the Necks of Others

Peter challenged the early church to refrain from the legalism that Jesus fought so fiercely. As the leadership debated whether non-Jews should be circumcised before being allowed to enter the church, Peter implored them: "Now then, why do you try to test God by putting on the necks of the disciples a yoke that neither we nor our fathers have been able to bear? No! We believe it is through the grace of our Lord Jesus that we are saved, just as they are" (Acts 15:10 –11).

Some followers of Christ are more adept at placing yokes than sharing them. Instead of focusing on our discipleship with Jesus, we place rules and regulations on others, creating the weariness and burdens from which Jesus tried to rescue us. We've all experienced legalism in the church; once movies, cards, and sports on Sunday were considered the taboos. Now alcohol consumption, worship styles, and how to dress in church are the practices scrutinized. In twenty years the list will be different, but the problem will be the same unless we start to focus on sharing our yoke with Jesus instead of placing our yokes on others.

Tell the Rest of the World the Rest of the Gospel

Let's tell the whole story. At our church, we have a little saying designed to encourage and motivate the people of our body to be active in their witness to Christ. We encourage everyone to set a goal each year: *Each one, Reach one, and Teach one.* All three parts of this phrase are crucial.

1. *Each one:* Sharing God's grace is everyone's job. Whether we have the spiritual gift of evangelism or not, we are all, as disciples, called to communicate God's grace. In the Old Testament, the blessing of the nations was carried out through the centripetal method—the drawn-into-the-center method. As God dwelt in the temple, He encouraged the nations to meet Him there. In Acts 1, Jesus changed the model to a centrifugal one—sent out from the center—telling His disciples to spread out across the globe, taking His message to the masses. He still expects us to do that today.

2. *Reach one:* The Holy Spirit saves people; we don't. God may have to carefully explain to us one day why He chose us as His instruments to communicate the gospel. At our church, we encourage our people to write the name of one to three people who don't know Jesus on a piece of paper and place it in a hole we have in our worship-center wall. This way, they are reminded every time they come into our church building that there are lost people who need to hear the gospel. We encourage them to pray for these people and share the good news with them. If someone says yes to Jesus, we place a rose on the stage so the whole church can celebrate. We also place the stories of these people on our Web page, Namesinthewall.com, to encourage our body.

3. *Teach one:* This is the rest of the gospel. We don't want to lead people to Jesus as though we were simply introducing some-one to a friend at a Christmas party. We want to introduce people to the yoke relationship to which Jesus has called them. So we disciple them and walk with them on their spiritual journey.

I have had the joy of meeting Billy Graham. What an honor and privilege to meet the greatest preacher of our generation. But he wasn't the biggest influence on my preaching. My mom and dad were my greatest influence. I lived with them, apprenticed under them, observed them, and sat at their feet and learned. Jesus doesn't just want to meet us; He wants to mentor us too.

Remember the lesson of this passage: If we want to find rest in our souls, we need to grasp the rest of the gospel. Once we learn this crucial principle, we need to share it with others. The only way we can focus on the yoke of mentorship with Jesus is if we pattern our lives around that goal and start passing on our secrets from the treadmill.

After each of our elder meetings, we have a prayer time, inviting the entire church to join us. Although not everyone heeds the invitation, we have a dedicated group of intercessors. We believe that our church continues to grow and succeed not because of our efforts, but because of prayer. Through a small yet mighty team, the works of the church are brought to God's attention. His Spirit breathes into these works and causes them to be life-giving because the load of the work is shared through intercessory prayer.

A business owner's wife from our fellowship was having trouble breathing. She went to a doctor who performed some chest X-rays and discovered a growth in her lungs and esophagus. In an attempt to cheer her up, I called her, and she cheered me up. God had given her a sense of abiding peace in the midst of this turmoil. Her husband was another story. Fearful and anxious, he was stumbling through the ordeal searching for any shred of hope. I found his reaction to be perfectly understandable and her reaction to be truly remarkable.

I invited them to the elder prayer time. This couple sat in two chairs while all the intercessors gathered around and laid hands on them. For half an hour we begged God to heal her and to give them peace. They were scheduled for a doctor's appointment two days later to receive the diagnosis. The night before the appointment, my friend couldn't sleep. In the dark near the bed where his wife slept peacefully, he talked with God. "I'll give You the business, Lord; I'll reprioritize my time; I'll give You my energy," he prayed.

Then the Holy Spirit whispered to his soul, "But will you give Me your wife?"

He wrestled honestly with the answer to that question and eventually relented, saying, "I trust You with her, Lord." He still didn't feel the peace he sought. Listening to the doctor the next day, he couldn't believe his ears. Although she had a serious ailment, the growth was not cancer as had been feared, and it was treatable. Talking with him after the appointment, he said, "God gave each of us what we needed. My wife needed peace, and she had it completely. I needed to have my world shaken up, and He shook it. I didn't need peace; I needed discomfort so I could get to the point of truly surrendering to Him."

When we are yoked with Jesus, He knows our needs and provides them, participating with us to bring us rest. We find peace in that realization.

Paradise Lost

Almost all of our sorrows spring out of our relations with other people.

—ARTHUR SCHOPENHAUER

There is no hope of joy except in human relations.

—ANTOINE DE SAINT-EXUPERY

E lijah had a second sabbatical. After great ministry he found himself exhausted, fearful, and depressed. *Christians aren't supposed to be depressed* is an anthem that's been sung in evangelical churches for too long. "If you would just trust Jesus, you would be happy all the time," we hear on television. I wonder what the TV preachers would have done had they run across Elijah, lying under a scrub bush in the desert near Beersheba, wishing he could die? "'Take my life; I am no better than my ancestors.' Then he lay down under the tree and fell asleep" (1 Kings 19:4–5).

Depression can cause us to isolate ourselves, just as it did Elijah. We may face the temptation to give up, even to the point of considering taking our own lives. Depression may cause us to sleep more than normal, lose track of time, and even forget from one moment to the next where we are going or what we are supposed to be doing.

My writing partner, Patricia Hickman, shared her emotional upheaval following the sudden loss of her teenage daughter, Jessi:

It was as though I were waking up and finding myself in a new hometown every morning. I got lost picking up my son's birthday cake at the neighborhood bakery where I bought his cake every year. On the drive home from church one Sunday, my son, who was ten at the time, asked me, "Where are we going?" I couldn't bear to tell him that I could not recognize any of the usual landmarks on our way home—I drove past the take-out chicken place, our bank, and finally wound up five blocks past the street that would take us to our house. Sensing my confusion, my son navigated us home, telling me where to turn until we finally arrived back in our driveway.

Time is the mender of such a broken-apart life. I began to take two one-week sabbaticals a year to a place where I could walk in nature, spend time in prayer, and write contemplatively in a journal rather than under the tyranny of a deadline.

She penned this piece while on a walk in nature:

I find a meadow green-smelling and wreathed by spires of winter evergreens. It took me by surprise. My eyes had lingered too long over thorn and thistle, making sore my climb into the rocky barrens. The birds filling the clouded sky had shared no good music with my human soul, but clamored noisily, only prosaic crows.

Wicked frost had killed the summer and left me without a song. Ignorance of the landscape had stolen my foresight and kept me climbing into the rocks and frozen climes, believing all the while the meadow did not exist.

But You, Sweet Wind, carried a green branch across the talus and dropped it on the treeless aerie where I labored.

I broke open the twig to smell its sap. I closed my eyes and imagined where I might find this place that fostered such life. I wanted to find its home.

I desired it. Desire is the smell of sweet longing, the awakening of the sojourner from night, the moon passing away to bow to the sunrise.

That is when my next step led me away from the thorn, away from the dead music of crows. Then my road-injured feet pressed against the soft green turf of pleasant pasturage and sent me a gentle thought, fresh moss's tome of comfort.

Oh, sweet meadow, you are not a lost dream!

The finches chirp like little girls upon the lawn, golden, as she was golden.

The daisies lift up their faces in expectation of reunions and the dance of the reunited.

It is wide and open here, and I can still see the rock distantly and remember that wretched climb through thorny bush. But that desolate place is now the dream and the meadow a pillow for my soul.

I sup here in the pleasant summer and know that I am finally home with thorns an olden pain.

> Can things in our lives be green again? We have accepted the winter of this world as the final word and tried to get on without the hope of spring . . . We have been so committed to arranging for our happiness that we have missed the signs of spring.
>
> —John Eldredge

Pain will always be a part of our journey. Like a winter that has overstayed its welcome, it can stretch long past our point of emotional breaking and leave us feeling hopeless. But how we long for those days when we find the meadow of comfort, drawn into it by the sweet wind of the Spirit.

I make no claim to being an expert on depression and other emotional struggles. However, I have seen a lot of depression over the years and have observed an emergence of several categories in the context of this internal struggle. Some people are depressed for physical reasons. It may simply be outright exhaustion but can go much deeper. There is no doubt that our bodies possess a delicate balance within a created chemical structure. As a result, in the ebb and flow of life's physical transitional periods, we can experience the rising and waning of our moods as well, with the possibility of postpartum, menopause-related, and a myriad of other depressions relating to anything from cancer to aging. As with all physical issues, we have doctors and medication to help us rebalance our systems and often get back on our feet, although medications do not always provide the perfect solution.

In a timeless account of his dying professor, Morrie Schwartz, writer Mitch Albom shared the interview between the ever-optimistic Morrie and Ted Koppel of ABC-TV's *Nightline* as they speak of depression:

> "Here's how my emotions go," Morrie told Koppel. "When I have people and friends here, I'm very up. The loving relationships maintain me. But there are days when I'm depressed. Let me not deceive you. I see certain things going and I feel a sense of dread. What am I going to do without my hands? What happens when I can't speak? Swallowing, I don't care so much about—so they feed me through a tube, so what? But my voice? My hands? They're such an essential part of me. I talk with my voice. I gesture with my hands. This is how I give to people."[1]

Dying of Lou Gehrig's disease, or ALS, Morrie Schwartz imagined a life without charity, and depression ensued. Giving of himself to others was Morrie's key to happiness, so the thought of losing what he felt was the essence of life—charity— depressed him. He mourned the loss of every part of his body as this debilitating illness progressed.

We grow accustomed to life as we know it. When we lose even a fragment of what have become our lives' habits, depression can seep in through the cracks of whatever is missing. For some it is a missing childhood, a loss of hugs, an absent father, a deficit of encouragement, or a vanishing dream.

The next category is moral depression, not a popular subject, but nonetheless a valid cause of depression. While our bodies were created to serve us and the world around us, we were also created with a conscience, making us higher than the animals and prone to feelings of guilt when we make decisions that cause grief.

Paul reminded us that the Holy Spirit is personal and, as a result, we can cause Him sorrow: "Do not grieve the Holy Spirit of God, with whom you were sealed for the day of redemption" (Eph. 4:30).

The Greek word translated as *grieve* means "to cause sorrow, pain, and distress." If the Holy Spirit lives in us, and we are causing Him sorrow, we will feel sorrow too.

In the sixteenth century, George Herbert penned these words to express the grief of sin:

> Lord, with what care hast Thou begirt us round! Parents first season us; then schoolmasters deliver us to laws; they send us bound to rules of reason, holy messengers, pulpits and Sundays, sorrow dogging sin, afflictions sorted, anguish of all sizes, fine nets and stratagems to catch us in, bibles laid open, millions of surprises, blessings beforehand, ties of gratefulness, the sound of glory ringing in our ears; without, our shame; within, our consciences; angels and grace, eternal hopes and fears. Yet all these fences and their whole array one cunning bosom—sin blows quite away.[2]

We climb over all of the fences surrounding us and find the grave of sorrow waiting for us. The Holy Spirit knows every thought we think. As a wise parent knows when a child is lying, the Holy Spirit knows all and sees all and is grieved when we lie to Him—as Ananias in the book of Acts lied to Him after secretly retaining part of the price of the land he had sold.

Hebrews 10:29 warns us that those who accept the gift of God's truth and then willfully turn their backs on it are insulting the Holy Spirit. First Thessalonians 5:19 warns us not to quench the Holy Spirit—a visual picture of dousing the fire inside us that lights our path. All of these sins cause the Holy Spirit sorrow.

> When God fills our inner vacuum with his Holy Spirit, life works. When God does not fill the vacuum, a host of consuming appetites swarm through our better intentions.
>
> —Calvin Miller

Then there is the sin of resistance: "You stiff-necked people, with uncircumcised hearts and ears! You are just like your fathers: You always resist the Holy Spirit!" (Acts 7:51).

Best-selling Christian author Terri Blackstock shared with us this personal account from her own life:

Back in 1990, my husband told me he wanted a divorce. Naturally, I plunged into a deep depression. But as I look back, I realize that my divorce was brought on because of sin in my own life. I was not walking with Christ in the way that I should have—I had been a selfish, self-centered, workaholic wife. Many times over the years, I felt God warning me that if I didn't change, I would lose my marriage. When it actually happened, I knew that I should have heeded that warning. Now it was too late. I repented of it, but I still had to suffer the consequences of that sin.

My depression continued for the next couple of years, and grew even deeper as I felt God's conviction that I needed to repent of some other sins. I was writing romance novels at the time—books full of graphic sex and profanity—and I knew that I was putting a stumbling block before my readers and causing them to sin. I grew more and more miserable as God kept convicting me. I tried to ignore it, and signed more contracts to write more books. But the more "successful" I became, the more miserable I became.

My depression did not fully lift until I finally surrendered the last holdouts of my life to Christ and repented of my sins. I got down on my knees and told the Lord that I didn't want to write another word that didn't glorify Him. From that moment, he began working in me in profound ways. I began to learn about dying to my self and living for God's glory. Since that time, I've written two dozen novels for the Christian market, and have seen God use my work to bear much fruit for Him. (From a personal conversation with Terri Blackstock)

My youngest son, Liam, is at the age where I have to tell him three or four times to do everything. "Liam, pick up your shoes and put them on the shelf, please," I say as he walks out of the kitchen, completely ignoring me. *"Liam, pick up your shoes and put them on the shelf, please,"* I say with a bit more volume, this time getting his attention.

"Why do I have to, Daddy? I don't want to," I hear from the living room.

"Excuse me, I don't remember asking you whether you wanted to or not. *Get in here now and pick up your shoes!*" The volume, the intensity, and the focus have all led Liam to believe that I am now serious about the request.

"No, I'm not going to do it!" he retorts as his four-year-old hands create a battle between Superman and a pink Power Ranger in the other room.

"Liam!"

"Okay, Dad," he finally relents.

His progression is from ignoring to refusing, rebelling, and then begrudgingly obeying. In this scenario, he resisted me, and it was very frustrating. When we resist the Holy Spirit, we do the same thing. We ignore His promptings and then tell Him why we don't want to obey. Finally, as the promptings persist, we tell Him we refuse to obey, until He makes it obvious that He means business, and we begrudgingly obey—sometimes.

Another kind of depression has nothing to do with our

chemical makeup or sinful patterns. It is the result of spiritual or relational forces. These forces can include oppression by forces of evil, sadness because of broken relationships, or loneliness. If these things beset us, all the medication in the world won't help, although it might make us feel a bit better, but the root issues remain.

Some Christians tend to blame all depression on moral reasons: "There must be sin in your life."

Secularists blame it on chemical reasons: "Let's just get you medicated, and you'll feel better."

Others are unaware of yet another category, the one that relates best to our hurry-sick lives. This is where Elijah's problem cropped up. Part of his problem was undoubtedly exhaustion. He ran one hundred miles to Beersheba. He was exhausted and famished. He was reenergized after eating and sleeping, so part of the problem was solved by sustenance. An angel brought him food, and he rested. Then the angel returned, fed him again, and said, "'Get up and eat, for the journey is too much for you.' So he got up and ate and drank. Strengthened by that food, he traveled forty days and forty nights until he reached Horeb, the mountain of God. There he went into a cave and spent the night" (1 Kings 19:7–9).

The difference between the exhausted and depressed man at the beginning of the text and the energized and productive man at the end of the text was—with nothing else apparent—a little sleep and nourishment. Sabbath. He stopped his work so he could see God's work. This wasn't the whole story, though. A more important sabbath waited around the corner.

A phrase from 1 Kings 19:3, "Elijah was afraid and ran for his life," can also be translated "He arose and went for his soul." Since in the next verse he pleads with God to take his life, he is obviously not afraid to die. He was not running from Jezebel because he was afraid to die. He ran to the desert because he knew he was dry and needed to spend "soul time" with God. After getting some physical rest, he was refreshed, and he ran again, this time 150 miles south to Mount Horeb. In the original text, the Hebrew direct article is used: "He went into *the* cave." This word emphasis leads commentators to believe that this was the same cave in which Moses had hidden when God appeared to him on the same mountain.[3] On that occasion, Moses asked to see God's glory, and God responded by allowing Moses to see His back while Moses crouched in a rock's crevice (see Exodus 33).

This cave was a special sabbath place, where two of God's great leaders met with Him. Moses was in the middle of a forty-day, forty-night sabbatical on the mountain with the Lord when this event took place. It is intriguing that it took Elijah forty days and forty nights to get to the same place—a little cave, all alone, where he could meet with God.

What happened in the cave leads me to believe that part of Elijah's depression problem was a moral problem. Even though his physical needs had been supernaturally assuaged, he still wasn't in the right place emotionally. When he arrived at the cave, God asked him, "What are you doing here, Elijah?" (1 Kings 19:9). This was God's gracious way of asking Elijah to pour out his heart. Jesus did the same thing on the road to Emmaus after His resurrection, when He saw two depressed disciples walking along.

> They stood still, their faces downcast. One of them, named Cleopas, asked him, "Are you only a visitor to Jerusalem and do not know the things that have happened there in these days?"
> "What things?" he asked. (Luke 24:17–19)

Jesus knew "what things," but He wanted them to talk. He wanted to listen and to invest time in the deep things with them. So they stopped walking and took a sabbath, sat down for a meal without the TV on, the radio blasting, the homework calling, or the telephone ringing, and were together. And in that quiet time, Jesus revealed Himself to them. Running back to Jerusalem, they told the other disciples what they had witnessed.

Even though God is all-knowing, He built into our makeup the need to transition into understanding, to mature, and to become better people today than we were yesterday. Confession, declaration, or admission is the vehicle He gave us for obtaining that transition. God doesn't want a bullet-point relationship with us; He desires prose. Long, detailed conversations sprinkled with provocative questions that drive us to the internal depths of our souls.

God also opened the door for Elijah to declare his fears, and he did: "He replied, 'I have been very zealous for the LORD God Almighty. The Israelites have rejected your covenant, broken down your altars, and put your prophets to death with the sword. I am the only one left, and now they are trying to kill me too'" (1 Kings 19:10). "Woe is me," he said. "I'm all alone. I've done a good job, mind you. *I have been very zealous for the Lord*, but it just isn't worth it anymore."

This is what we might call a "prophet pity party" in the presence of God. It leads me to believe that the root of Elijah's depression was moral. The sin of self-centeredness had overtaken him. The fact remained that many other prophets were loyal to Yahweh, but his pity blinded him to them. Even though he was in the presence of God Himself, he struggled. The honest answer to God's question should have been either "I was afraid of Jezebel, so I ran as far from her as I could get" or "I am so desperate for You, and I knew I could find You here." Instead, he played the martyr and piously reminded God of his passion. God knew what he needed: "The LORD said, 'Go out and stand on the mountain in the presence of the LORD, for the LORD is about to pass by'" (1 Kings 19:11).

He needs to have an encounter with Me, as did Moses, years ago, on this same spot, God thought. The way God passed by is the primary lesson of 1 Kings. Read the following carefully:

> Then a great and powerful wind tore the mountains apart and shattered the rocks before the LORD, but the LORD was not in the

wind. After the wind there was an earthquake, but the LORD was not in the earthquake. After the earthquake came a fire, but the LORD was not in the fire. And after the fire came a gentle whisper. When Elijah heard it, he pulled his cloak over his face and went out and stood at the mouth of the cave. (vv. 19:11–13)

God doesn't speak in loud ways. He doesn't write His name across the sky with clouds or burn His initials into cornfields with fire from heaven. Nor does He send an earthquake tearing the crust of the earth to form a presentation of the gospel written with reconfigured asphalt streets. God whispers! The word translated *whisper* in the text is disputed by Hebrew scholars. It actually means "inaudible sound," but a whisper is the quietest such sound translators could find to use.

Bernie Krause records nature sounds for movies and for song sound tracks. Rob Bell tells us that in 1968, Krause required fifteen hours of filming to log one hour of uninterrupted time without the modern disruptions of airplanes, car sounds, or train whistles. By contrast today, two thousand hours of recording are required to tape one uninterrupted hour of nature's music.

Libby and I were test-driving minivans recently and discovered separate sound and DVD systems for the passengers in the backseats—designed so that we each can listen to our own noise and not have to bother other passengers, often family members. Most of us have cell phones, pagers, voice mail, multiple TVs, and radios that blare constantly.

One cell phone commercial portrays a haggard old cowboy leaning over the railing of his fence, shaking his head because his pasture is full of dachshunds. "I just don't know what happened," he gloomily reports. "I called on my cell and asked for two hundred oxen, and they sent these things." A man in a long trench coat puts his ear to the man's phone and verbalizes a prevalent problem of our age—static.

Even when we finally turn off the electronics, we fill our lives with silent noise: crammed schedules, newspapers, magazines, and the Internet. If we serve a God who whispers, and our lives are full of noise, our chances of hearing Him are lessened to the tenth power.

Gary Thomas said, "Our sin is that we passively rebel against God, filling our lives with so much noise and busyness that God's voice cannot, or will not penetrate."[4] Thomas has led me to a theory. I am convinced that knowing God speaks in the quiet, we fill our lives with diversions. We are actually intimidated to hear what He might say to us if we do quiet our lives.

What parent can't relate to Thomas's scenario of calling his kids in from playing for ice cream, resulting in instant obedience, only to call them in for dinner to find a stunning lack of response?

"We didn't hear you, Dad!" they claim, after you have yelled "Dinner" for the third time. Instead of answering, "Forget you, Dad, we're playing!" they pretend not to hear. We are too programmed by our decorum to say to God, "Forget it, God, I'm enjoying myself" when He calls us to deeper commitment or painful decisions, so we ignore His gentle whispers by filling our lives with the sweet treats of noise. Pascal wrote, "We should not need to divert ourselves from thinking about it (the voice of God)."[5]

Our culture barks demands from the tumult as our God whispers to us from the wind. To stop the competition takes an act of the will on our part. Actively, we stop and listen.

Finally, Elijah's noise-filled life was miles behind him, so he heard God when He said: "What are you doing here, Elijah?" God was plying Elijah to share his heart with Him, since He had initiated the encounter by sharing Himself with Elijah. God goes first. He whispers to our souls when we quiet them enough to hear, and then longs to hear back from us.

My friend's eighteen-year-old son calls me on my cell phone periodically to ask me biblical questions. Early one morning, he called to ask, "Where does it say in the Bible that you can't take it with you?" I simply couldn't remember the text and had to hang up without giving him an answer. This troubled me. I wanted to

give a drink to this thirsty student. I went out on my deck immediately after flipping my phone closed and sat down to read my
Bible. At the time I was reading through the Psalms, one per day.
I opened my Bible to Psalm 49. Asking God to speak specifically
to me, I read until I got to verse 16:

> Do not be overawed when a man grows rich,
>   when the splendor of his house increases;
> for he will take nothing with him when he dies,
>   his splendor will not descend with him. (vv. 16–17)

God's desire to communicate His truth and heart to me was
evidenced in an instant when my desire sprang from a thirsty
student's request. God's Word draws us to Him; we respond; He
answers again. He hopes to hear that we've grown by spending
time with Him, that we've developed in our walks and our attitudes have taken a U-turn. Elijah responded: "I have been very
zealous for the LORD God Almighty. The Israelites have rejected
your covenant, broken down your altars, and put your prophets
to death with the sword. I am the only one left, and now they
are trying to kill me too" (1 Kings 19:14).

When we are despondent, we think selectively. We focus on
certain aspects of our lives and neglect everything else that is
going on. As Alexander Maclaren wrote: "Despair is always
color blind; it can only see the dark tints."[6]

The Lord had seen Elijah's despondency caused by physical
exhaustion and self-pity. But might we discover a deeper reason
for it? Could there be loneliness, or a spiritual or relational reason dogging us?

Christian author Eric Wiggin shared with us a personal struggle
with unforgiveness: "My own experience with depression involves
holding a grudge against a guy who had bullied me in high school.
I had nightmares for years, often followed by outbursts of anger.
These all vanished when I laid the matter on the Lord and truly
forgave the guy."

Could it be that even though Elijah wasn't alone, since there were more than one hundred prophets being protected by Obadiah, he *felt* alone? Many of us have experienced being at a gathering in a room full of people and feeling desperately alone. I think this was God's thought process. He didn't reprimand Elijah for his self-pity; He immediately resolved the loneliness that caused it: "Anoint Elisha son of Shaphat from Abel Meholah to succeed you as prophet" (1 Kings 19:16).

God wasn't replacing Elijah. If we continue to read the story, we find the reverse was true. In 1 Kings 21, God still used Elijah for effective ministry. God still rained fire down from heaven when Elijah asked for it (see 2 Kings 1:10). God still did amazing miracles through him (see 2 Kings 2:8), and the Holy Spirit didn't pass to Elisha the cloak of Elijah until Elijah had gone into heaven on a whirlwind (see 2 Kings 2:15). God wasn't punishing Elijah for his sadness; He was providing relief from it. If Elijah felt alone, God wanted to provide companionship for him. The best way to do so was to provide an apprentice who would spend each day with Elijah and learn from him.

It is not that God always heals depression. That simply isn't true. Sometimes He intervenes, and other times He doesn't. The point is that Elijah's true need was discussed and brought to the front when Elijah ran to the desert to meet with God. When Elijah quieted his voice, he could hear God's whisper.

This happened in a powerful way when Libby and I headed to Wisconsin for our four-week break. Years earlier, after our second child, Annika, was born, Libby struggled with postpartum depression. We didn't realize she was struggling with this depression, assuming instead that she was tired, overwhelmed with having two kids in eighteen months and relocating our church.

We felt she would soon snap out of it. But she didn't. Off and on over the next seven years, Libby continued to struggle with depression. We could usually find a reason for it, and we rarely called it by name. Yet it remained. One of the reasons that Libby was so excited about our family sabbatical was because she longed for extended husband time—time when I was wholly present.

After a week of ministry at a favorite camp, we settled in for two weeks of nothingness at a friend's cabin. The setting was spectacular. A magnificent lake, canopied trees, verdant lawns, a pasture to play all kinds of games with the kids, two soft chairs to sit in under the trees while reading, kayaks, canoes, and, most importantly, nothing on the schedule. We woke up each morning and asked the same open-ended question: "What shall we do today?" It was fabulous. We had loads of fun riding bikes on an old railroad-turned-bike-trail, swimming in quarries, hiking through rolling nature trails, smelling the wildflowers in the butterfly garden, and spending time with our extended families.

One evening Libby and I were talking in the family room. She looked sad and finally confessed that she was sad. She said, "I'm getting a little scared." I asked why. She said, "I assumed that if I could just get us all away from the rat race for a little while, I would start to feel better. But I don't. How could I still be depressed when I'm living in paradise? I've got your full attention, the kids are doing great, we are having more fun than should be allowed, we're staying in a quaint cottage, and I still feel down and gloomy."

We talked at length and agreed to pray together for the remainder of the rest time. Near the end of our time in Wisconsin, she announced, "I've made a decision. I've decided that if I'm still depressed in a place where all my circumstances are ideal, my depression obviously isn't circumstantial." Now, this makes sense, but it took a run to the desert and an encounter with God in the cave to figure it out. "So what are we going to do?" I asked.

"I'm going to get some help."

When we returned home, Libby connected with a counselor—an older, wise woman—and simply said: "I was in paradise, and I was still depressed; what is going on here?" They started to meet weekly, and Libby talked openly and frankly. One evening she told me that a theme was starting to appear in her discussions with Kathy: "My mom keeps coming up."

Libby's mom is one of those people everyone should know. In fact, if you live in southeastern Wisconsin, you most likely do. In all my life I have never met anyone like her, and there are few people I respect more. She was radically saved out of a life of alcoholism when Libby was eighteen months old. She threw herself into her walk with Christ with a tenacity that would be very difficult to maintain. She still passionately preaches Christ each Sunday afternoon at the nursing home, where she rehashes the pastor's morning sermon as she has for more than thirty years. She counsels struggling believers, stops gossip in its tracks, and maintains a presence in her church of ten thousand that few people miss. Dottie is a gem.

"Your mom?" I asked. "Really? What are you thinking?"

Libby shared with me some of the painful aspects of her childhood for which her mother was responsible. Nothing illegal or horrendous, but nevertheless painful. My heart sank as I listened.

"I'm going to invite my mom down for a weekend, have her sit down with Kathy and me, and I'm going to share my pain with her, share my forgiveness with her, and pray that God gives us the relationship I've always longed for. I think this is one of the root causes of my internal struggle, and I long to make it right."

This trek took an enormous amount of courage on both Libby's and Dottie's parts. But they went into the weekend with open minds, and God did an amazing work. Libby wrote a typed, single-spaced, seven-page letter to her mom, sharing with her the painful aspects of her early years. This is how it started:

Dear Mom,

I pray that this time will be blessed by God. I am so glad we both know and love Him. The reasons why I want to talk with you are:

1. I see you as a rich blessing that I am missing out on in life because of barriers that we both built many years ago.

2. I love you so much and I grieve at the drop of a hat at the thought of losing you. I feel that I have been taking you for granted. I desire that our relationship would be characterized by freedom, peace, and enjoyment of each other for the rest of our years together.

3. In the past eight months that I have been in counseling, I have learned a lot about myself that I previously couldn't see, even though I was desperately seeking God for the answers to my mental anguish. I have realized that some of my walls that are hindering me now were built with the habits that I developed to cope with my life growing up. I want God to control me. Not negative patterns or walls.

4. These walls I've skillfully crafted are holding me back in my ability to love others, function freely in the ministry, parent, communicate in marriage, value my dear friendships, sort out my own feelings, to feel again, and to celebrate the things that are worth celebrating in life . . .

5. God compelled me to write this. He is making it happen. I fully trust that He will work in these days . . .

It was an agonizing exercise. Thoughts of betrayal and fear of verbal injury almost caused her deep regret at having initiated the encounter. But she so desperately wanted to heal the relationship that she persevered with tears and wrote every necessary word. Dottie arrived, the Holy Spirit filled the discussions, tears were shared, forgiveness granted, grace given, grievances buried, and out of the ashes, a spark kindled a relationship anew.

As we sat on the deck after the second day of talks, I witnessed a miracle. I heard melody in the voices and charity in the responses. I saw tears of laughter and smiles of joy. They had always had a working and adequate relationship, but now—now real life emerged!

When Elijah got into the cave with God, God touched Elijah in his despondency. When Libby got into an emotional cave, she became aware of her despondency. In both cases, God provided relational grace.

When we stop our work, we see God's. Sometimes what God wants to work on is our own hearts and souls. When our lives are too loud, we can't hear the whisper. When we do hear the whisper, we'll hear Christ revealing Himself to us and revealing ourselves to us as well. We must discipline ourselves to turn down the volume of our lives, slow down the pace of our lives, and remove some of the stuff in our lives that pads our walls but keeps us from hearing the solutions.

Jesus said He came that we might have a full life, not a filled life. There is a huge difference.

John Ortberg, speaking at a Willow Creek Association conference of children's ministry volunteers and staff members, agreed:

I'm going to be a different person this year. Starbucks sales are going to go down dramatically this year. Because when I wake up in the morning I'll be so rested that having a cup of coffee will be like throwing kerosene on a raging fire. There are going to be vacant office chairs after business hours; there's going to be empty seats on business class in airplanes because I didn't take trips that would mean being away from my family. There's going to be open rosters on peewee soccer teams because parents have decided that they will not bow down before the golden calf that is North American junior soccer. When your perfectionist mother comes to your home, you will invite her to write the word *joy* in the dust on the coffee table. You will remind her that dusting is in fact only small particle rearrangement, and you will tell her that one day on your tombstone it will read, "Big Deal, I'm Used to Dust."

You are ready to commit right now no matter what opportunities this means passing up. No matter what promotions you have to watch go to some less deserving person than you. No matter what aspect of your lifestyle you have to downsize. No matter who it means you have to disappoint. No matter what legitimately good achievement you have to miss out on, you're ready to live a simpler saner life, even if it costs you money and makes people mad at you and feels kind of boring and gets you fired.

Amen.

When you take a sabbath rest and find you've lost your hope for paradise, spend time with the Christ who wants to hear your deepest, darkest fears and to nurse your meanest wounds. He is shaping you into His image, one that will not erode or need a nip or tuck at the end of the next decade. True paradise is constructed at the hands of a Master Builder. He will work with you, molding you and shaping you with the utmost of patience. He will take His time with you, knowing the finished work is beyond our visible horizons and knowing that He began such a work first, inside you. You were created to connect with your Creator. But you are continually being fashioned as part of something grander than the life you see in front of you. You are a work of craftsmanship, tooled as one part of a greater whole.

Custom-Made for a Different World

9

Blessed are the single-hearted, for they shall enjoy much peace. If you refuse to be hurried and pressed, if you stay your soul on God, nothing can keep you from that clearness of spirit which is life and peace.

—AMY CARMICHAEL

For in this we groan, earnestly desiring to be clothed with our habitation which is from heaven.

—2 CORINTHIANS 5:2 NKJV

New ministries in the Carolinas have often had to face the fact that the people of this region are skeptical of any new works shrouded in spiritual idealism. This is in great part due to the failure of a famous ministry that fell under the weight of national scandal and disgrace. The plan sounded perfect, ideal—a Christian paradise complete with a family theme park, miles of shopping, and a beautiful residential village—a virtual utopia for Christians. With signs like "Heavenly Ice Cream" hanging over the doors of the shops, Christians flocked to offer financial support to this thriving ministry with the promise of having a piece of the dream. The failure of this mega ministry, and the lost revenues of the husbands, wives, and grandparents who supported it, will live on in the annals of Christendom as the utopia that never materialized.

It is within this modern mishmash of faith and greed that we can be lured into believing it is possible for us to create a perfect world on Earth, one in which we can live in perfect bliss and harmony. It is, we believe, an honorable desire. But God never intended the longing He placed inside us to be a self-fulfilling aspiration. Deluded by desire, we can force ourselves to live in frustration, longing for a place on Earth that will never exist. It does exist, however—but not here. Because our life here will never be ideal, neither will we find the perfect rest while weighted down in a vessel of clay.

I am a gifted sleeper. When I lay flat, my body checks out. When the alarm goes off, it feels as though I had just lain down. The kids don't wake me, the dog doesn't wake me, and sometimes my alarm doesn't wake me. Perception management would require me right now to tell you the reason I sleep so well is because I work so hard, or because I have a clear conscience. The truth is, I sleep well whether I'm working hard or not.

Periodically I will have a bad night. It goes something like this: In the middle of the night I hear something downstairs. Looking over at Libby sleeping soundly, I reach for my three-iron that I keep under the bed. Then, grasping it firmly, I walk slowly toward the door. Opening our bedroom door, I see shadows moving through the lace-draped windows in the front of the house. Slowly walking down the stairs, I arrive at the landing with my back to the wall. It is quiet now. As I continue toward the first floor, I hear scratching on the front doorknob. My heart races. From this central vantage point, I can check all three kids' rooms and find relief in the stillness found there. I see the phone on the counter and grab it as I walk by. The scratching has stopped now. I breathe deeply and shuffle toward the door. My plan is to look through the peephole, and if I see anything wrong, I will punch "call" on my phone, which will dial the previously entered 911 number for me.

The scratching starts again. It sounds so low on the door now, it could be a cat, dog, or even an opossum. As I close my right eye and lift my left eye to the spy-hole, my heart sinks as I see a huge man in black charging the door. I have no time to respond as the door crashes in and lands on top of me. The gruesome intruder holds his hand over my mouth as I try to scream, desperately fearful for my life and my family's well-being. Suddenly I hear Libby's voice breaking through the mayhem: "It's all right! Wake up; it's a bad dream!"

I find myself wrestling with my wife in bed, dripping sweat, my heart pounding, and my fears eating me alive. Sitting up, I look at the clock and find it is two o'clock. It is Sunday morning and I've had another nightmare. I lie awake through the dawn with images in my mind and adrenaline coursing through my body. As nights go, this is a bad one.

We all experience both good nights and bad nights. A good night's rest is a gift, often taken for granted until it doesn't occur. Bad nights can be caused by nightmares, depression, stress, a full mind, and even excitement—like a boy anticipating his first early morning fishing trip.

We can take time off that turns out to be a bad rest for any number of reasons. One of the problems with finding a sabbath rest is that we are forced to enjoy it in the midst of a fallen and painful world. Many attempts to connect with God and enjoy His presence meet with failure, frustration, and disappointment. We are disappointed in this life because we were created for something much better. He has "set eternity in our hearts," and as a result we long for something greater than can be experienced here on Earth (see Ecclesiastes 3:11).

C. S. Lewis is often quoted in regard to our otherworldliness: "If I find in myself a desire which no experience in this world can satisfy, the most probable explanation is that I was made for another world."[1]

This other world is also inhabited by humans housed in bodies made for another world. Our souls, the part of us to which God presently chose to not make us privy, are the reason we long for another place. Because we cannot see our own souls, we forget they are the quintessence of who we are and of our most honorable aspirations. The soul sparks the fires of our hearts' cries, fanning into flame the longing we experience for eternal things. The dream of eternity is a badge stitched upon the soul's heart that reads "Not Home Yet."

I have known this longing standing on a frozen summit. It was one of those trips of which dads dream. Two of my dear friends, their two boys, and my son Cameron and I set off for the mountains of New Mexico for three days of skiing. Because of schedule conflicts, we were forced to leave in the evening and drive through the night. We arrived in Amarillo, Texas, around two in the morning, and it was my turn to drive. As soon as I took the wheel, the snow started.

By the time we crossed the border into New Mexico, the road was completely covered in white powder. Snow iced the nighttime landscape in a silvery mantle. The two-lane highway was impossible to see but for the reflectors on the road's shoulders—my only guides. One truck passed us in the four hours that I drove. Since no one else was foolish enough to be on the road, I put my left front tire in his tire track and prayed that he had stayed on the road. We couldn't see thirty feet in front of the car. Driving at the crawl of thirty miles per hour, my eyes never left the road and my hands never left the steering wheel. My friend took over for me, and the snow worsened. As we wound our way into the mountains, concern overtook my thoughts.

The snow finally started to level off. The plows came and cleared the roads. From the cloud cover, the sun peeked out and we saw the ski hill on the horizon. The three dads cheered; the boys woke up. We could all but taste our relief. Later that day we found ourselves on the mountain summit, pristine blue skies overhead, brilliant sunshine warming our faces, and a wide-open mogul run below. I thought: *This must be a little of what heaven is like.*

I can write those words for you, but you have to be on top of that mountain to experience the sense of beauty after having known its dark and icy side at night. To understand the traveler's price to observe such splendor gives us room for pause. To know God's rest often comes at great cost.

It reminds me of the apostle John, who, having experienced exile, is caught off guard when suddenly handed an eyeglass to see into eternal things. Recording the radiance of heaven, we sense a near-frustration in Revelation 4 as words failed what his eyes beheld. Notice how he used the words *appearance* and *like* in the following descriptions: "And the one who sat there had the *appearance* of jasper and carnelian . . . Also before the throne there was what looked *like* a sea of glass, clear as crystal" (Rev. 4:3, 6, italics added).

We know the frustration of being handed a glimpse of eternity through the eyes of this apostle. It makes us hungry for eternity now. The weariness of life can overtake our thoughts, and our longing for another world can become our misery, when God intended this promise of a better place to be our rest.

Sometimes from our desperation God gives us a moment of unprecedented peace, beauty, adventure, or camaraderie where we think: *It really doesn't get any better than this*, and then He whispers into our hearts, "Oh, but it does, and I can't wait for you to experience it!" In the meantime, we are traveling down a road, knuckles white with tension, eyes glued to the path to ensure safe passage, possessed of a dream we imagine as the summit of sabbath rest.

While the skiing was fantastic, one of the things that made the journey wonderful was the struggle we went through to arrive at the summit. The moment we left the driveway we were "on the ski trip," but the full joy of the trip truly hit home when the trials were behind us and the trails were before us. In the same way, Christians experience eternal life the moment they trust Jesus for salvation. Eternal life is qualitative, not simply quantitative. We trust Jesus, and He gives us *rest for our souls*, but as we live with Jesus in the difficulty of sojourning through a fallen world, the prospect of the *best rest* becomes our hope instead of our despair.

In Hebrews 4 the author gives a stern warning. The original recipients of this pamphlet were Jews who had heard the gospel and had renounced Judaism, but many still did not trust in Christ. The modern equivalent would be churchgoing moral people who look right, sound right, dress right, even give right, but in actuality are not right with God.

To this group, the author of Hebrews uses the people of Israel as a negative example. Rescued from slavery by God, they were always longing for the "good old days" in Egypt. With their heads turned back to Egypt and their bodies walking toward Canaan, they were aptly described as "stiff-necked people" (Ex. 32:9). The defining moment for them occurred in Numbers 13 and 14, when they sent a special force of twelve to map out the promised land prior to the celebratory conquest.

The problem occurred when ten of the men came back afraid and poisoned public opinion against the leadership. Two men, Joshua and Caleb, stood firm, spoke with faith, and challenged the people to stop whining and strap on their swords and fall in line: "God promised! We're here; let's go!" The fear of the people trumped the preaching of the fearless, and the people rebelled. God's anger burned against the people, and they were told that they would all perish in the wilderness and miss out on the *rest* of the promised land. Caleb and Joshua were the exceptions because they had trusted God and were prepared to move forward (see Numbers 14).

Hebrews 4 begins: "Therefore, since the promise of entering his rest still stands, let us be careful that none of you be found to have fallen short of it." *Therefore* reminds us of the preceding passage, where we find the failure of the children of Israel described in haunting terms:

Who were they who heard and rebelled? Were they not all those Moses led out of Egypt? And with whom was he angry for forty years? Was it not with those who sinned, whose bodies fell in the desert? And to whom did God swear that they would never enter his rest if not to those who disobeyed? So we see that they were not able to enter, because of their unbelief. (Hebrews 3:16—19)

Therefore, because this *missing out* is possible, and because the promise of rest still stands today for the church, we must be careful that we don't miss out. This *best rest* or *sabbath rest* is a synonym for *eternal life*, the abundant, full life that lasts forever. It means lying down, settling in, being fixed and secure. It includes being confident and feeling free to lean on Christ for everything. It leads to a blissful audience with the King of kings that lasts one day longer than forever. It is full, and fully satisfying. It is Christ himself in us, the eternal One. But some people will miss out.

The author of Hebrews said, "Let us be careful that none of you be found to have fallen short of it. For we also have had the gospel preached to us, just as they did; but the message they heard was of no value to them, because those who heard did not combine it with faith" (Heb. 4:1–2).

They had good news preached to them. Their good news focused on the physical offering of God's grace, a land "flowing with milk and honey." We, too, have heard the good news. Our good news is aptly translated as the *gospel*—the message that Jesus, fully God and fully man, shed His perfect blood as a sacrifice for our sins. We have heard that by trusting in His death and inviting the risen Christ to live within, we would be saved, transformed, reborn, and given a new start. We've heard it all before. But like the people of Israel, some of us have not received the free gift of sabbath rest.

If the fast-food chain McDonald's made a generous offer to give away free hamburgers on June 1 in celebration of kids being out of school, we might all think, *How nice of McDonald's*. They could advertise the giveaway in every venue known to man. But the fact remains, unless I go to the nearest McDonald's on June 1 and receive my free hamburger, the whole promotion would be meaningless for me. As it was for the Israelites, the good news would be *meaningless* for the simple reason that I *did not combine it with faith.*

People today say how nice it is that Jesus died for the sins of the world. But they forget to ask Him to cleanse them. Sabbath rest, the *best rest*, is secured by faith. Faith is simply living as though the Bible is true. So when Jesus says, "Come to Me and I'll wash your sins away," we believe He will do it, and we submit accordingly. As the passage continues, we see the two options available to people today: "Now we who have believed enter that rest, just as God has said, 'So I declared on oath in my anger, "They shall never enter my rest"'" (Heb. 4:3).

Those of us who have asked Christ to save us from our sin enter true rest. Those who do not trust in Christ alone for salvation will never enter true rest. This is the truth of the gospel, both sides of the coin, and it all hinges on faith: "And yet his work has been finished since the creation of the world. For somewhere he has spoken about the seventh day in these words: 'And on the seventh day God rested from all his work'" (Heb. 4:3—4).

There is a hint at the type of rest being described in the qualifier "*my* rest." We enter into the rest God enjoys. Not by sitting down from exhaustion or laziness in the middle of the day, but the rest of a work finished. It is the feeling we embrace when standing back from our flowerbed with intense feelings of joy after a day of work on our knees. It is the godly pride that wells up as our eighteen-year-old strides across the platform, throws her hat in the air, and dances toward adulthood. It is the ecstasy of closing on the house, burning the mortgage, or handing over the reins to the young replacement.

The *best rest* is described in terms of completion. As the text continues, however, we see that the propensity to procrastinate the decision to trust Christ is a foolish one: "It still remains that some will enter that rest, and those who formerly had the gospel preached to them did not go in, because of their disobedience. Therefore God again set a certain day, calling it Today, when a long time later he spoke through David, as was said before: 'Today, if you hear his voice, do not harden your hearts'" (Heb. 4:6—7).

The "long time later" refers to the time lapse between the events of the conquest recorded in the book of Joshua and the time of the psalmist. David reminded us in Psalm 95 that God calls us to respond *today* to His offer of grace. Procrastination leads to a hardening of the heart, which means it will be more difficult to receive the grace at a later date.

"For if Joshua had given them rest, God would not have spoken later about another day" (Heb. 4:8). "Joshua" is an appropriate translation of the Greek name, but in the original language, *Jesus* and *Joshua* are the same. Joshua apparently failed to give the people of Israel the *best rest*, but Jesus came to offer that gift to all of us. The story of Joshua and the promised land sheds necessary light on this passage from Hebrews.

There is a debate among evangelical scholars as to the application of the ultimate sabbath rest found in Hebrews. Some would argue that the promised land is a symbol of heaven. Thus the people who are hearing the gospel but not responding to it are nonbelievers who forfeit the opportunity to spend eternity with God. Others would say that the promised land represents the blessings God has for Christians in this present life. So, the people who hear the gospel but do not respond to it are on the outside of God's blessings for today. I'm not convinced we need to argue.

When I recall the conquest of the promised land, I think of it in two stages. In the first stage, the next generation of God's chosen people arrived in a land flowing with armies and soldiers. War was the order of the day. There was certainly a portion of rest, but the battles still raged. The people who entered the promised land had to wait until ultimate peace was found. In the same way, we also must wait for our definitive rest.

The time of true peace arrived when all the enemies were defeated and true peace ruled. In the first eleven chapters of Joshua, war raged, people died, and the people of Israel defeated their foes. Finally, the Word says in Joshua 11:23, "the land had rest from war"—the summit under blue skies. When this came true, "heavenly" rest arrived—described like this:

> So the LORD gave Israel all the land he had sworn to give their forefathers, and they took possession of it and settled there. The LORD gave them rest on every side, just as he had sworn to their forefathers. Not one of their enemies withstood them; the LORD handed all their enemies over to them. Not one of all the LORD'S good promises to the house of Israel failed; every one was fulfilled. (Joshua 21:43–45)

Characterizing this ultimate rest for the Israelites is a *complete defeat* of enemies and a *complete receipt* of blessings. This tranquil state, however, is merely a symbol of the spiritual rest God wants to give people today.

In returning to Hebrews, we find: "There remains, then, a Sabbath-rest for the people of God" (Heb. 4:9). The *best rest* is ours to enjoy and ours to share. All around us, sitting next to us in church, and even serving next to us in ministry are people who are lost because they have never truly trusted Christ for salvation. Some of you reading this book are sensing a strange warmth in your body. A question appears in your mind: *Have I ever really handed myself over to Jesus?* Even though we say we believe in grace, some of us are still trying to work our way to heaven.

"For anyone who enters God's rest also rests from his own work, just as God did from his" (Heb. 4:10). We enter the *best rest* by resting from our best efforts. We must stop trying to impress God with our Christian activity and comprehensive ministry. In his book *What's So Amazing About Grace?* Philip Yancey taught us:

> There is nothing we can do to make God love us more—no amount of spiritual calisthenics and renunciations, no amount of knowledge gained from seminaries and divinity schools, no amount of crusading on behalf of righteous causes. And there is

nothing we can do to make God love us less—no amount of racism or pride or pornography or adultery or even murder. Grace means that God already loves us as much as an infinite God possibly can.[2]

He loves us perfectly, right now. Our performance, both positive and negative, is completely irrelevant to Him. Our positive performance doesn't impress Him: "All our righteous acts are like filthy rags" (Isa. 64:6). And our negative performance is covered by the blood of Jesus: "We all, like sheep, have gone astray, each of us has turned to his own way; and the LORD has laid on him the iniquity of us all" (Isa. 53:6). Performance cannot enter the picture. God in His perfect love offers us the *best rest*, and our responsibility, by faith, is to take it. *Today* is the best time to say yes.

"Let us, therefore, make every effort to enter that rest, so that no one will fall by following their example of disobedience" (Heb. 4:11). An example of disobedience, or disbelief, is the Israelite men and women who perished in the wilderness because they refused to trust God. Caleb and Joshua represent those who say yes to God and enter the *best rest* called *sabbath rest*, or eternal life.

To understand the person who has tasted this sabbath, we can listen to Caleb's energized dialogue. Notice Caleb's age along with his fire. After watching his entire generation wilderness-wander for forty years while waiting to die, he said:

Now then, just as the LORD promised, he has kept me alive for forty-five years since the time he said this to Moses, while Israel moved about in the desert. So here I am today, eighty-five years old! I am still as strong today as the day Moses sent me out; I'm just as vigorous to go out to battle now as I was then. Now give me this hill country that the LORD promised me that day. You yourself heard then that the Anakites were there and their cities were large and fortified, but, the LORD helping me, I will drive them out just as he said. (Joshua 14:10–12)

Caleb resounded, "God promised it to me, so I'm moving in!" He was eighty-five years old, strong, feisty, captivated by the promise of God, motivated to see those promises become a reality, and activated to make God's name resound through the hills. The fierce army that opposed him was irrelevant. He had entered the land. True sabbath rest energizes people to make a dent in the territory held by Satan while waiting for the hope of glory promised in Scripture.

I know a modern-day Caleb. His name is Major Ian Thomas. As a young man, he discovered that by handing himself fully over to Christ, Christ would live His life through him and make a supernatural impact through him. He has been traveling the world preaching this message for more than sixty years now. He is in his early eighties and is as feisty a man as ever. Recently he was talking with my father over a cup of tea. Eyes afire with passion he said, "Stuart, the Iron Curtain is rising, the continent of Africa is wide open to the gospel, the church is exploding in South America, the good news is spreading through the Far East . . . Don't you wish you had another life to live?"

Major Thomas's taut resolve, emblazoned with the message of the gospel and at the same time so embedded with the hope of glory, is part of the struggle of living the sabbath rest before we enter the *best rest*.

In 2002, Libby, Cameron, and I went on a four-day trip to Bolivia with Compassion International. While we were waiting for our return flight I got sick. After twenty minutes, I was worried I was going to die. Twenty minutes later, I was worried I wouldn't die! I still had about seventeen hours of travel ahead of me. The flight to Miami was agonizing. I passed out in the hallway at Miami International Airport, so a friend plopped me into a wheelchair and whisked me toward our connecting flight. We got bogged down in customs and missed the flight. An airport official asked me if I had requested the wheelchair through the correct channels. I replied that I hadn't. He told me I had to get out and wheeled my transportation away. So as I lay down on the floor of the terminal, hurried travelers walked around my prone body, while Libby tried to secure comfortable passage home.

My friend said, "Pete, you need to get up!" I asked him why, and he answered, "Because they'll think you're sick if you don't!"

"I am sick; I really feel this bad!"

"Yes, but they won't let you on the plane if they think you are too sick," he responded.

So I stood up, wobbled to the nearest pillar, leaned against it, and tried to paste a halfway realistic smile on my pea-green face. We caught a flight to Dallas that was mostly empty so I lay down on three seats. I am six feet five inches tall, and I didn't fit very well. The seat belts dug into my rib cage. I was still nauseous, my head ached, and my intestines churned. I rested, somewhat. After our arrival in Dallas, we walked to the car, loaded the luggage, and drove to our house. I was completely exhausted. I left Libby with the bags, stumbled up the stairs, turned on the light, and gazed at my bed. I lay down, and rested.

On the plane from Miami to Dallas I had rested somewhat. It was imperfect, frustrating, and at times painful, but it was better than no rest at all. But when I got home, I truly rested. As we make our way through this life, we will rest imperfectly, but it is better than no rest at all. One day, however, we'll be home.

In the days and weeks that followed the loss of her daughter, my writing partner, Patricia—a Christian mother, author, and pastor's wife—grappled with what she knew to be the place of rest called heaven:

> I had always found great comfort in thinking of heaven as the place where my Savior lived and waited for me. But now, tackling the shocking news that my too-young-to-die daughter now waited for me, left me feeling anxious about eternity—had she truly crossed through that mysterious veil peacefully, did she feel lonely crossing over without me, was she being cared for as lovingly as I had cared for her? All of the things I knew to be true about

heaven had somehow been shattered loose by what seemed a cruel snatching away by unseen hands.

Finding continued peace and rest in thoughts of eternity had to be preceded by a faith not founded on happy affirmations. We know them all by heart—don't worry, trust Jesus; heaven's just another country; real Christians don't face despair.

I had to reexamine my beliefs, beliefs shaken to the core, and stick upon broken stick, reconstruct what I had to know was reality.

I studied the Scriptures not just for descriptions of heaven, but for the texts pointing to the character and nature of the One who had ushered Jessi into eternity. I had to understand at least a shred of the mystery of God's godness in order to rest in completely trusting Him again.

My precious friend who speaks at the Women of Faith conferences, Marilyn Meberg, offered her loving counsel and then asked if I, from the grotto of grief, had settled the issue in my heart regarding the sovereignty of God. I knew the correct answer by heart—that God is sovereign. But trusting His sovereignty had become my test of the hour.

To grasp a full portrait of God that I could look on with the same spirit of surrender I had experienced before my daughter's death, I had to know Him more deeply. It was in that reaching that I found a hand reaching back.

Throughout Scripture, from Genesis to Revelation, was one constant. In my human state of variableness was an immovable unvariable—my only anchor.

I had been led against my will into a dark cave. It was lightless and airless and I could feel it sucking the life from me, knowing I was being dropped into the darkness, into the bottomless pit of despair—if it had not been for one thing—the vigil of Jesus. He never left my side. It was from my inward cave that I cried out to Him from the pit, and felt that scarred hand slip around my own, leading me ahead from the light of His own heart.

That is when I realized my privileged state, having God as my personal guide through the pit—slime-bottomed, snake-writhing place that it was—to wade through together, sharing the secrets between us that had battered my faith, created to Creator, and know a spiritually birthed assurance that can come only from the personage of Jesus. I could tell Him the worst things about myself, and He spoke back to me in the language of grace.

I had wanted it my whole life—to hear the Voice of God. I simply did not know the ticket to the inmost cave would cost so much.

It was from there I set out with my little bag of pain in one hand and the nail-scarred hand holding on to the other, privileged and aching to get to the other side; praying the next leg of the journey would be short, yet knowing pain would add to the contents of the bag again before my journey was finished.

My longing for a better place was bolstered in knowing God's rest because I know God better. I know that God, because of His paternal nature, can still be trusted to sojourn with me on my way and to give me a rest that surpasses all earthly sense of rest.

We were not made for this world. From its ragged, gasping deathbed, the creature longs to reconnect with the One who breathed life into its nostrils, gave it a mind with which to think, and a will on which to act. We must, today, reach from the cave of our unrest and find the hand reaching back for us.

It's your move—trust Him; give yourself fully to Him. From an act of your will, long to know Him better, experience the blessing of absolute surrender and, in confidence, join with the saints in the prayer of the ages: *Come, Lord Jesus, come.*

The Things
We Don't Do Anymore

10

Stop and listen to the heart, the wind outside, to one another,
to the changing patterns of this mysterious life. It comes
moment after moment, out of nothing, and disappears into
nothing. Live with less grasping and more appreciation and
caring.

—JACK KORNFIELD

In order to seek one's own direction, one must simplify the
mechanics of ordinary, everyday life.

—PLATO

The good ol' days are overrated. Nostalgia can cloud our
otherwise clear hindsight, causing us to remember the
past with a sense of romance. I reflect back on my early childhood in England with great fondness. I ran around the fertile
countryside, threw chestnuts at my friend, dodged cow pies, and
pretended to be a knight as I scaled the walls of Capernwray
Hall to joust with unsuspecting sheep.

My selective memory neglects to remind me of the cold,
damp "middle lodge" where we lived between two other English
lodges leading into the Hall's property, each lodge "guarding a
gate." One was an upper lodge, the other a lower lodge, and in
the middle, our home—the drafty old middle lodge.

An ancient coal-burning stove was our only source of heat. I
remember sliding into the cold linens on wintry nights and waiting for my body heat to help warm me beneath the bundle of

blankets my mother had given me. At sunrise my siblings and I ran for the only bathroom, our feet tiptoeing across the icy floors in the morning as the frost coated the drafty windowpanes.

My father traveled around the United States the majority of the year to preach. I recall that as a boy I felt a sense of pride in my dad's work, but also a sense of loss in his absence. I had only one or two toys I called my own—by today's standards a veritable toy deficit.

While growing up in an English countryside comes with its own romantic setting, I cannot say that I call those days "the good old days." Most of us, even if we cherish the way things used to be, would never go back to "the good old days." By the same token, we tend to think that life is better now because of technology, opportunity, and ingenuity. But is life really better now?

Anne Lamott, in her provocative memoir *Traveling Mercies,* retold the story of a man who was dying of lung cancer. Stunned at his resolve and positive outlook in the midst of such dire prospects, she said, "He's so savoring the moments of his life right now, so acutely aware of love and small pleasures that he no longer feels that he has a life-threatening disease. He now says he's leading a disease-threatening life."[1] I wonder how I would cope if my doctor called to tell me my life expectancy had been shortened? I wonder if I would live a "disease-threatening life"?

Libby and I flew to a conference a few months ago. As I reflected on our trip one morning, I started to think about the potential danger of flying in this day and age. I imagined the plane rapidly descending after a loud bang blew out an engine. I mentally dramatized how Libby and I might look at each other—shocked and realizing that someone else would rear our children. In the midst of planning my memorial service, I was struck by the reality of my own mortality. I pondered the thought: *If I could live my life over again, how would I live it?*

I penned in a journal how life would be different if I knew I was going to die soon, or if I had been diagnosed with a terminal illness. The things on my list, the things I would change if I were disciplined enough, are mostly things we simply don't do anymore, things we once did when we valued sabbath rest more highly. The fact remains that we are all terminally ill. The Word tells us that we are all destined to die, and then face the judgment (see Hebrews 9:27). Some people have less time to live than others, but as each day passes, we all are one day closer to the end. Let's think back to the "good ol' days," the simple days, when *sabbath* meant something, and reflect on the treasures we have lost.

Back before radio, digital television, Pong, Nintendo, Game Cube, Walkman, Game Boy, computers, palm devices, cellular phones, instant Internet access, sports leagues, gymnastics, summer camps, ski trips, the Shopping Channel, and ESPN—people read books. Not that I can remember those days. I am a product of the information age. I can't write legibly on paper because I am keyboard-oriented.

But my father tells me of a time in the not-too-distant past when Sunday was special, revered. His parents held a rigid view of the Sabbath that he would not necessarily purport. But the other end of the spectrum, where most of us dwell, is no less dangerous. My dad's family enjoyed a day of rest, a time of reflection, a breather in an otherwise full life every week.

What kinds of things did they do in those seemingly archaic days? They read good books; they sat on the porch taking pleasure in thoughtful conversation, stealing naps, sitting around the table for family meals, attending worship together as a family, and devoting themselves to a family time of Scripture reading. They played board games, took Sunday drives, went for walks, and built crackling fires in the hearth. They took long, hot baths, told the children stories, and went to bed early.

Isn't it stunning how few of these restful activities we still do? The Sunday drive has been replaced with a soccer mom's suburban ritual drive to the playing field. Books have been traded for electronics. Conversation has been obliterated by television, naps are for lazy people, and mealtimes are sacrificed at the fast-food altar. Family worship has been replaced by segmented ministry where the whole family is in the church building, but everyone is in different rooms. Board games collect dust in the attic. Walks in the park take too long, so the kids ride their scooters while the parents lose touch. The hearth has been supplanted by the realistic fire video—it is so much cleaner. Long, hot baths give way to quick showers. Stories around the coffee table cannot be heard because parents don't tell them. What would be the point? Kids are now wired up to earphones anyway.

Some of these lost riches are cultural and some are biblical. There are at least three lost treasures that biblical characters cherished: reading, writing, and simplicity.

Reading—The Joy of Gleaning

The early childhood of Jesus was described in these well-known words from Luke 2:52: "Jesus grew in wisdom and stature, and in favor with God and men." The context of this statement was the evening His parents discovered Him discussing issues of theology with the teachers in the temple. Jesus knew the law. He studied it, memorized it, quoted it, and read it.

In his book *Brothers, We Are Not Professionals*, John Piper said: "My spirit does not revive on the run . . . Few things frighten me more than the beginnings of barrenness that come from frenzied activity with little spiritual food and mediation."[2]

What else feeds the soul like reading? God chose to communicate to us through a spoken word that was translated to the written page. The book became God's choice for specific self-revelation. The last century has given way to the stardom of dynamic duos in the entertainment world—Simon and Garfunkel, Crosby and Hope, Lewis and Martin, Lucy and Desi, and Siskel and Ebert. When one died, the other continued—but not like before. All were capable entertainers or communicators by themselves. A special synergy ignited, however, when these duos came together. Their art in tandem remained legendary.

The Holy Spirit is responsible for our spiritual growth. He teams up with a partner—Scripture—to make an unbeatable force. Learning to listen with a sense of openness to what the Spirit says to us through Scripture takes us into higher paradigms of God's wisdom—and His rest.

In his book *Scribbling in the Sand*, Michael Card said:

> We are to listen with as few presuppositions as possible, coming to the Word with the same sort of openness we might offer a friend who has let us know they have something important to tell us . . .
>
> When we find ourselves trying to listen to someone whose speech is slow or deliberate, the great temptation is to finish their sentences for them. The same is often the case when we listen to God's Word, particularly to those passages with which we think we are familiar. But one of the great proofs that Scripture is alive is its ability to speak afresh through passages I thought I knew by heart. In fact, I might have known them by "head," but not until they came alive in the heart had I really begun to listen.
>
> Adopting a listening stance before the Word means keeping your mind as quiet as possible and letting the Bible finish its sentences, its stories. This will bring a new freshness into your time with the Word.[3]

The Holy Spirit is the great translator, who acts as He wills upon our sitting-down moments where we stop to open up one of the many Bibles lying around the house. When we set aside a part of the day to hear from God, be it when we awaken at dawn or before we lay down at night, it is like connecting our lives to the Wisdom of the Ages. I imagine this magnificent energy source coursing with knowledge, existing and operating within us, breathing life into our yielded spaces—a privilege I cannot quantify with human words.

Philip Yancey wrote: "The Spirit cannot be kept like a personal pet, living in a small compartment somewhere inside us to be brought out at will . . . The Spirit is not a homunculus banging on pipes for our attention but rather an indwelling part of the entire building. The Spirit does not act on us so much as with us, as a part of us—a God of the process, not a God of the gaps."[4]

In his classic booklet *Balanced Christianity*, John Stott explained the tendency of evangelical Christians to polarize.[5] Over the years, the issues change, but the inclination persists. When embracing the partnership between the Bible and the Holy Spirit, some Christians chase after the extremes. One end of the spectrum is unfettered enthusiasm, or neglecting the truth of God's Word in lieu of an emotional spiritual experience. Donald Bloesch said, "Whereas in the first part of the 20th Century the Holy Spirit seemed to be the missing person of the Trinity, this is now more true of the Father."[6]

I noticed a book section in a Christian bookstore labeled "Charismatic Issues." Titles filled the shelves with thousands of pages speaking about the experience of the Holy Spirit in the Christian walk. This in essence is a positive emphasis, unless the believer becomes so enrapt in experience that the foundational truth of God's Word is compromised. One need simply watch some of the TV preachers to see steady instances of manipulated doctrines.

On the other end of the spectrum is unmitigated formalism, or neglecting the work of the Spirit for systematic textual evaluation. Sound dry? There's good reason. Thomas Torrance described this mind-set: "The Bible is treated as a fixed corpus of revealed prepositional truths which can be arranged logically into rigid systems of belief."[7] The historical tendency of the Bible church movement is to analyze the text, synthesize the thesis, and proclaim the proposition—thus making God's living Word dry, crusty, dusty, and dead. The Bible is not simply the declaration of propositions. It involves a personal address by a living God. Donald Bloesch says, "Evangelical rationalism needs to be superseded by a biblical evangelicalism that respects mystery in faith yet is adamant that meaning shines through mystery."[8]

Desiring to understand and employ God's Word in our lives, we have two choices:

1. To be enthusiastic biblicists, or

2. To be biblical enthusiasts

The views are the same, of course. The church needs a unity of *logos* (word) and *pneuma* (spirit). Jesus said we are to worship in Spirit and in Truth—life is worship. We are to live in the constant cradle of these two bound entities.

> All this I have spoken while still with you. But the Counselor, the Holy Spirit, whom the Father will send in my name, will teach you all things and will remind you of everything I have said to you. (John 14:25–26)

As the Holy Spirit teaches us, He uses the Word of God, which He inspired; He illumines the truth enabling us to recall what we've read (see 2 Timothy 3:16; and Ephesians 1:17–19). But we cannot recall a Scripture that is not embedded somewhere in our neurons. We would be wise to follow in the footsteps of Jonathan Edwards, who resolved to be a Word-saturated man: "Resolved: To study the Scriptures so steadily, constantly, and frequently, as that I may find and plainly perceive, myself to grow in the knowledge of the same."[9]

The Bible does not stand alone in relaying God's heart to humanity. The themes of Scripture lie behind a large percentage of great art, including literature.

One spring our family vacationed in Hot Springs, Arkansas. We stayed in a lovely home. I played golf, we enjoyed the towering trees, and each morning I rose early to read. I lounged in a padded rocking chair and opened pages penned by my favorite author. As the sun peeked through the trees, spreading warmth into the silent house, Charles Dickens transported me to London and Paris. *The Tale of Two Cities* so arrested my soul that I arose on the last morning well before five o'clock, possessed of a desire to finish the story. My pulse quickened as I read of Sydney Carton sacrificing himself so another might go free—freely offering his head to the guillotine while the undeserving man ran to his freedom. I thought, *I am that man*. It came to me: *Jesus did that for me*. The story of the Atonement rang clear as crystal upon my quieted heart. I wept as the power of His sacrifice rested upon me and left me immobilized by truth.

Victor Hugo's classic *Les Misérables* is another potent example of the message of Christ speaking through story. Jean Valjean, a poor man sentenced to jail for stealing bread, wasted away for years in a draconian lockup. While traveling to another jail, he spent the night in the home of a vicar. During the night he slipped downstairs, filched a sack full of silver, and escaped. Early the next morning, the vicar was roused from his sleep by two uniformed police officers holding Valjean by the neck. "Look what we found, Vicar," they said, proudly holding up the bag of stolen silver. The vicar, in one of the greatest demonstrations of grace in all of literature responded, "Oh, I'm so glad you found him. He forgot these!" Removing two silver candlesticks from the mantle, the vicar added them to the bag of stolen goods.

The officers took their leave, and the two of them are left standing alone—Valjean speechless on the doorstep. He left, a new man touched by a grace giver. From this turning point in the story, we see the vicar's grace multiplied in Valjean's heart. He runs a factory with grace; he cares for the orphaned daughter of a prostitute with grace. Having received, he freely gave.

Valjean's nemesis, Javert, was driven by law. He was the officer from the prison who could not rest until Jean was once again behind bars. Javert chased him throughout the story, finally cornering him in the city streets. As the two central characters struggled, Valjean got the upper hand. With one twitch of his finger, his weapon could end the life of the antagonist. Instead, Valjean remembered the grace shown to him. He dropped his weapon and walked away. We can almost hear the story whisper:

Once you've received grace, you're compelled to give it. Javert could not understand Valjean's mercy. He refused to receive Valjean's gift of humility and jumped to his death in defiance. Law bludgeoned grace, and grace drowned law.

In his article "The Good News According to Twain, Steinbeck, and Dickens," Mark Storer encourages us to find Jesus embedded in Steinbeck's *The Grapes of Wrath*. The character Jim Casey (note the initials), personifies God's heart for the downtrodden. Storer says that great authors such as Dickens, Flannery O'Connor, Leo Tolstoy, Simone Weil, and William Carlos Williams "are simply retelling the Bible, albeit sometimes in a way that makes some Christians angry."[10]

Whether we are reading God's Word, the classics, fiction, or nonfiction, the act of drawing our thoughts into a realm that causes us to stop and reflect upon our own hearts, our flaws, charity, those who are different from us, or simply a good story that takes our minds off self-centered worrying, a book stands as the greatest tool for leading us into a moment of reflection and rest.

I long believed that reading required large blocks of time. Because the precious commodity of time is hard to come by, I often pushed aside my reading time as a lesser priority. John Piper helped me tremendously when he said, "Suppose you discipline yourself to read a certain author or topic twenty minutes a day, six days a week, for a year. That would be 312 times 12.5 pages [at the modest rate of 250 words a minute] for a total of 3,900 pages. Assume that the average book is 250 pages long. This means you could read fifteen books like that in one year."[11]

Since some of the great masterpieces are much longer than 250 pages, and since reading the great historical works is a wise priority, we could find ourselves reading a great book like John Calvin's fifteen-hundred-page work *Institutes* in twenty-five weeks.

Piper goes on to quote a lengthy section from C. S. Lewis's work *On the Reading of Old Books* that includes these timeless truths: "It is a good rule after reading a new book, never to allow yourself another new one until you have read an old one in between." Lewis explained his adamant belief in this reading balance: "We all . . . need the books that will correct the characteristic mistakes of our own period. And that means old books." The section concludes: "The only palliative is to keep the clean sea breeze of the centuries blowing through our minds, and this can be done only by reading old books."[12]

Reading old books is important, but reading biographies about great thinkers is equally enriching. "Good biography is history and guards us against chronological snobbery (as C. S. Lewis calls it)."[13] When I read a few years ago the biography of Dawson Trotman, the man who founded the Navigators, the mediocrity of my walk with Christ manifested as an observation in the written page—the patterns of a man sold out to Christ. It is one thing to desire to be sold out. It is a much richer experience to observe someone doing it, gleaning habits and disciplines that enrich and fortify our faith. While reading the life stories of Billy Graham, John Adams, and even Douglas MacArthur, I have learned in both positive and negative examples what it means to lead, live, and love well.

Writing—The Joy of Journaling

What would we know of the plight of Jews during the Nazi invasion if Anne Frank had not sat at her small table each day and recorded her thoughts? Of course, behind the highly publicized story of Anne Frank rests the primary fear of journaling: we're convinced someone (or more than one person) might read it one day.

Journaling is a sabbath activity that provides enormous benefit and receives minimal attention. King David's journal was published, and it is found in our Bible as the book of Psalms. The writings of Solomon, Luke, John, Paul, and Jeremiah all contain the thoughts and prayers these men committed to paper.

David Brainerd, George Müller, George Whitfield, and Jim

Elliot all recognized journaling as a crucial aspect of their daily walks. Many people are aware of Jonathan Edward's "Resolutions," a written description of the personal reform he desired to embrace. What many people don't realize, however, is that he chronicled his progress in these areas each day in his journal.

As Donald Whitney records in *Spiritual Disciplines for the Christian Life:* "More than almost any other discipline, journaling has a fascinating appeal with nearly all who hear about it. One reason is the way journaling blends biblical doctrine and daily living, like the confluence of two great rivers into one."[14]

Maurice Roberts implored us to return to the practice of Sabbath days past, when he said, "No one will keep a record of his inward groans, fears, sins, experiences, providences and aspirations unless he is convinced of the value of the practice for his own spiritual progress. It was this very conviction which made it a commonplace practice in earlier times."[15]

I am content. I sit down at my desk, a bare kitchen table with a blotter, a bottle of ink, a sand dollar to weigh down one corner, a clam shell for a pen tray, the broken tip of a conch, pink-tinged, to finger, and a row of shells to set my thoughts spinning.

—**Anne Morrow Lindbergh, *Gifts from the Sea***

Journaling helps us note our progress or regress to follow our lives' patterns, noticing the footprints we left behind in both validity and impact. Journaling provides concentration so that we can meditate without our minds wandering. It allows us to express our deepest feelings, whether exhilaration or despondency. Writing our lives on paper reminds us of the powerful works God has done on our behalf, so we can say with Asaph:

"I will remember the deeds of the LORD; yes, I will remember your miracles of long ago. I will meditate on all your works and consider all your mighty deeds" (Ps. 77:11–12).

As Francis Bacon said, "If a man write little, he had need have a great memory."[16] Whitney concludes, "An old adage says that thoughts disentangle themselves when passed through the lips and across the fingertips. While reading makes a full man, and dialogue a ready man, according to Francis Bacon, *writing* makes an *exact* man"[17] (italics added by author).

I first learned about journaling when reading Bill Hybels's book *Too Busy Not to Pray*. Hybels, the senior pastor of Willow Creek Community Church, struggled to reduce his human RPMs. He could not slow down the pace of his life to hear the still, small voice of God. One day, while reading a book by Gordon McDonald, he discovered a simple approach to journaling that assuaged his concerns about "people spending hours and hours in the middle of the day just letting their stream of consciousness flow all over endless reams of paper."[18]

McDonald suggested starting a spiral notebook page with the word *Yesterday* and then recording "a little description of the people you interacted with, your appointments, decisions, thoughts, feelings, high points, low points, frustrations, what you read in your Bible, what you were going to do and didn't."[19] McDonald suggested limiting the writing to one page, requiring condensed thought and protecting against unhealthy introspection. Hybels discovered that doing this simple exercise "will reduce our RPMs from ten thousand to five thousand."[20]

I cannot say, with Hybels, that I journal every day. As in the rest of my spiritual disciplines, I am inconsistent and somewhat sporadic in my journaling. However, I can say that when I follow this simple exercise, I hear God's voice.

When I started my sabbatical, I bought a leather-bound book with nothing written in it. I sat down each morning to write about *yesterday*. Early one morning I was reading Robert Benson's quaint reflection called *Living Prayer*, specifically his chapter titled "Dancing on the Head of a Pen," in which he describes the value of journaling. After reading, reflecting, and recommitting myself, I wrote this entry:

> 7-19-01
>
> Today I finished reading *Living Prayer*, the chapter about jour-naling. It was good. Reminded me that no one else is ever going to read this, it doesn't have to be profound, and that, "The Journals are one part history, one part prayer, one part confes-sional, one part meditation, one part storage facility, one part discipline, one part hope."[21] Buechner wrote "It is as though each day is a treasure hunt and a journal is one way of seeing if you found the treasure God has hidden for you this day."[22]
>
> I long to slow my life when I return home. I long to deepen my walk, develop my prayer, dwell in the Word, start my day this way. Lord, help me do these things, I love it when we are together!

Not very profound, not beautifully written, not really worth publishing. But two years after I wrote it, I was able to open my journal, turn through a few pages to find the entry, read it through, and, in the process, be reminded of my personal resolve as I was transported back to the red-and-green couch in the fam-ily room of that rustic cottage where I connected with God in a precious way.

Simplicity—The Joy of Less

One of the distinguishing characteristics of my grandparents' home was its simplicity—decorative whatnots, connected to a memory instead of a color scheme, graced time-loved tabletops. Free of all modern distractions, a sabbath rest inside those unde-manding walls was possible. One of the great ironies of our day is that the technology we have produced in order to simplify our lives has made our existence more complex by providing more options. The family spreads out around the house, each multitasking, channel flipping, or instant-messaging. As options increase, simplicity flees to the dark corners of the house, poking her chaste face around the edge of the wall only when other options run their course.

In 1999, an e-mail chain mailing attributed to "unknown source" grabbed my attention:

> The Paradox of our time in History is that
> We spend more, but have less;
> We buy more, but enjoy it less.
> We have bigger houses but smaller families;
> More conveniences, but less time;
> More medicine, but less wellness.
> We read too little, watch TV too much, and pray too seldom.
> We have multiplied our possessions, but reduced our values.
> These are times of tall men, and short character;
> Steep profits, and shallow relationships.
> These are days of two incomes, but more divorce;
> Of fancier houses, but broken homes.
> We've learned how to make a living, but not a life;
> We've added years to life, not life to years;
> We've cleaned up the air, but polluted the soul.

Walter Kerr wrote a book called *The Decline of Pleasure* in which he tracked the lack of contentment in our present culture. With great insight he concluded: "We are all of us compelled to read for profit, party for contacts, lunch for contracts, bowl for unity, drive for mileage, gamble for charity, go out for the evening for the greater glory of municipality, and stay home for the weekend to rebuild the house."[23]

He is challenging our propensity to do things as a means to an end, instead of doing them simply for enjoyment. Everything we do is utilitarian. With utilitarian activity, educational opportunity, financial security, familial intensity, ecclesiastical quantity, technological proclivity, and cultural conformity, is it any wonder that complexity has plundered simplicity? When our lives, minds, souls, and schedules are full of so many fillers, we become incapable of recognizing the happiness found in minimalism.

Sherlock Holmes and Dr. Watson went on a camping trip, set up their tent, and fell asleep. Some hours later, Holmes awakened his faithful friend. "Watson, look up at the sky and tell me what you see."

Watson replied, "I see millions of stars."

"What does that tell you?"

Watson pondered the question: "Astronomically speaking, it tells me that there are millions of galaxies and potentially billions of planets. Astrologically, it tells me that Saturn is in Leo. Time wise, it appears to be approximately a quarter past three. Theologically, it's evidence the Lord is all-powerful and we are small and insignificant. Meteorologically, it seems we will have a beautiful day tomorrow. What does it tell you?"

Holmes, silent for a moment, then spoke: "Watson you idiot, someone has stolen our tent!"

Like Watson, modernity can blind us to the obvious elements stolen right from under our noses—the need for rest. Whether we are blinded because we're trying to make our lives more secure, more profitable, or more pleasurable, the deficit we cause in our lives or our families' lives is canyon-sized.

Centuries ago, Pascal addressed human inclination when he said, "All our life passes in this way: we seek rest by struggling against certain obstacles, and once they are overcome, rest proves intolerable because of the boredom it produces. We must get away from it and crave excitement."[24]

The root of the problem is that excitement is our primary value. In actuality, many of the best things in life are far from exciting on the surface. Certain portions of a Dickens novel can be painful and sluggish. Journaling can fire the kindling of grief, tents can get wet, and family dinners can prove argumentative and frustrating. With cries of "boring" echoing through the home, we acquiesce and upgrade the toy that was working fine a few minutes ago, creating the charge of adrenaline that doesn't last as long as the last one.

Simplicity has a conjoined twin. Wherever we find simplicity we also discover contentment. It is the lack of contentment in our daily options that drives us to lead complex lives. Contentment is the prescription for the disease of compulsion. Paul addressed both twins in 1 Timothy 6:6–10. He encouraged Timothy to lead his people to a place of contentment: "But godliness with contentment is great gain. For we brought nothing into the world, and we can take nothing out of it" (1 Tim. 6:6–7).

Life is a journey from one moment of nakedness to another, so we should travel light and live simply. "But if we have food and clothing, we will be content with that" (1 Tim. 6:8).

Wound up in this simple fisherman's anecdote is found the yearning for contentment:

A fisherman relaxed on a beach in Mexico. A brash American tourist happened by and asked why the man wasn't at work. "I've finished my work for the day," he responded.

"At one in the afternoon?" the American incredulously responded. "Why don't you go out and fish some more? You could catch more fish."

"Why would I want to do that?" the man replied.

"Because then you could make more money."

"What would I do with that?"

"You could buy more fishing boats."

"And then what would I do?"

"You could expand your business and buy a refinery on the coast."

"Really, and why would I want to do that?"

"So you could make lots of money and retire."

"What do people do when they retire?"

"They buy a place on the beach and sit around and do nothing!"

"Well, that's what I'm already doing!" the wise fisherman concluded.

How hungry our lives become to truly understand the tender underbelly of an old Chinese saying:

> We never buy more than we need.
> We never need more than we use.
> We never use more than
> It takes to get by
> Till we learn to need less.

Paul said, "People who want to get rich fall into temptation and a trap and into many foolish and harmful desires that plunge men into ruin and destruction" (1 Tim. 6:9).

"For the love of money is a root of all kinds of evil" (1 Tim. 6:10). Not money itself—materialism is not the possession of material things, but the unhealthy obsession with them. "Some people, eager for money, have wandered from the faith and pierced themselves with many griefs,"verse 10 continues.

Bishop John V. Taylor summarized Paul: "Our enemy is not possessions but excess. Our battle cry is not 'nothing,' but 'enough.'" Can you say "enough"? Contentment is saying each day, "I have enough. What God has provided for me is adequate, if not exorbitant, and I am not going to seek more. I am going to make a conscious effort to live a lifestyle below what I am capable of living, to wear last year's clothes, to share hand-me-downs with my friends who have children the same age as mine, to hold on to electronic devices until they wear out, to unplug the video games during the school week, to refuse to upgrade perfectly good appliances, to stay in my house as it 'gets smaller' with growing children, to pay cash for used cars, and to give generously with what I save as a result."

A few years ago, I read a true story about a millionaire and his wife who decided, after committing their lives to Christ, that enough was enough. They gave up their million-dollar home for a cheaper one in a quiet subdivision. The journalist who interviewed them was surprised to find that in preparation to entertain her, they had prepared a meal of soup and bread. They told the writer that they ate soup and bread at every meal, finding it healthy and inexpensive. The money they saved on a simpler lifestyle, they gave away to the poor and to missions. They confessed how happy their lives had become by giving up the things they once thought so important.

Paul concluded his section: "Command those who are rich in this present world not to be arrogant nor to put their hope in wealth, which is so uncertain, but to put their hope in God, who richly provides us with everything for our enjoyment" (1 Tim. 6:17). Notice he didn't tell them to sell everything. He actually encouraged them to enjoy their blessings. But that isn't the end of this admonition: "Command them to do good, to be rich in good deeds, and to be generous and willing to share. In this way they will lay up treasure for themselves as a firm foundation for the coming age, so that they may take hold of the life that is truly life" (1 Tim. 6:18–19).

The life that Jesus wants us to enjoy is not driven by the desire for a new form of excitement. The life He longs for us to live is found in enjoying each day, realizing we have enough, and sharing generously with those in need. How do we do this? Paul gave us the secret in Philippians:

> I am not saying this because I am in need, for I have learned to be content whatever the circumstances. I know what it is to be in need, and I know what it is to have plenty. I have learned the *secret* of being content in any and every situation, whether well fed or hungry, whether living in plenty or in want. I can do everything through him who gives me strength. (4:11–13, italics added)

The secret is that I can do all things through Jesus, who lives in me. Libby and I have asked Jesus to give us the gift of contentment, a prayer He has answered. One of our great joys is sensing our "enoughness," rejoicing in pleasure in our home. We bought the house twelve years ago before we had kids, hoping to "grow into it."

More than a decade has past. Three children have been added to the mix, and they're getting bigger. A playroom, a study, and larger bedrooms would all be nice, since we have no basement. But a God-given contentment assuages those desires. We recently bought an inexpensive wrought iron canopy and placed it on our deck. When we built the deck we planted a sapling in the middle of it and cut a hole around it. Now the tree covers the deck. The canopy, complete with potted plants, fits snugly under the out-stretched branches, providing a comfy get-away as we look out over the lovely golf course that a nice contractor built behind our house a couple of years ago. We had to wait for the tree to grow to get the full benefit, but in the waiting we found great benefit in both our pocketbook and in simple pleasures. Our "starter home" is enough. We may one day move, and when we do we will have peace in doing so, but contentment is a blessed gift.

A couple in our church have taken God's teaching about simplicity to very pragmatic conclusions. The wife, Sue, sent me the following e-mail:

A few years ago, we lived on Oakbluff Circle, the house with the pool and three yards. After a few years of upkeep on this high-end house, someone said to us, "Oh this is beautiful; you must really enjoy it."

We talked later and decided as pretty as it was, we did not enjoy it, because it took all our time and money to maintain it. We were going broke and were always so busy and overwhelmed. We did not feel that was the quality of life we wanted. Quality family time was so scarce. The boys were growing up so quickly, and we felt that our life had become consumed with keeping up our stuff.

So we sold the house, moved into an apartment, and when our son moved out to go to college, we downgraded even more to another apartment in Plano. We will buy another house in the near future. But it will be small, with very little yard.

What we want in life has dramatically changed.

Two years after making this move, Rob got meningitis and one year later, July 2002, he was laid off after seventeen years of faithful service to his company. While a shock to both of us, the loss of his job has been manageable with our lower cost of living. We simply have no worry about the future. We both have complete peace.

Even with the drastic change that came into our lives, our quality of life has been awesome. We spend so much less time and money that we have more time for each other and our sons. We experience a freedom that is beneficial to our contentment, and we no longer feel like we are on a financial merry-go-round. Our sons do not seem to be materialistic and are great young men.

Sue's story reverberates with the contentment that she and her husband have found in simplifying.

In her famous sabbatical's journal that eventually became the critically acclaimed work *Gift from the Sea*, Anne Morrow Lindbergh said:

I mean to lead a simple life, to choose a simple shell I can carry easily—like a hermit crab. But I do not. I find that my frame of life does not foster simplicity . . . The life I have chosen as a wife and mother entrains a whole caravan of complications . . . for life today in America is based on the premise of ever-widening circles of contact and communication . . . My mind reels with it. What a circus act we women perform every day of our lives. It puts the trapeze artist to shame . . . This is not the life of simplicity but the life of multiplicity that the wise men warn us of. It leads not to unification but to fragmentation. It does not bring grace; it destroys the soul.[25]

My heart echoes Lindbergh's sentiments. What I mean to do, I do not. Paul understood our frustration too: "For the good that I will to do, I do not do; but the evil I will not to do, that I practice . . . O wretched man that I am! Who will deliver me from this body of death?" (Rom. 7:19, 24 NKJV).

Are we then intended to wander our lives hobo-style, carrying everything we own in one ten-ounce bundle? By all means not, yet within us is a yearning for less that wars with the hunger for more. By beginning with the Spirit's call—that voice that beckons us away from the desert of materialism into the meadow of life in the Spirit—we can then examine what is necessary against what is cumbersome under a pure light, casting away the chaff to keep what is golden. Embarking on that kind of journey, we can find freedom from the manacles we long to leave behind.

I have no desire to go back in time fifty years. We live in the most exciting time in history. If we can keep excitement in its proper place, as a gift of God and a fleeting treasure, and elevate contentment and simplicity to their rightful place as foundational for the abundant life, we will be shocked to discover that we have time for "the things we don't do anymore."

No Wonder They Call It Holy

The image of Jesus Christ and my own image will be coalesced into one. I will experience what I've been saying is the hunger of life: union with Jesus Christ. How ever does God fix the categories? Whatever does heaven look like? Whatever is the great mystery of godliness? We must leave it all to his keeping. The important thing is, we have a chart! We have a destiny!

—CALVIN MILLER

But ours is the long day's journey of the Saturday.

—GEORGE STEINER

There are great days and there are *great* days. Great days are those moments when everything seems to fall into place. The spouse is happy, the kids bring home A's, the client buys, the tax man refunds, the body shrinks, the bank account grows, the soul is nourished, and the brothers and sisters in the body are served. Jubilation (great) days have nothing to do with our jubilation; they have everything to do with Christ's provision. These "red-letter days" all point to the redeeming work of Jesus: Advent, Christmas, Epiphany, Ash Wednesday, Palm Sunday, Maundy Thursday, Good Friday, and, of course, Easter.

Maundy Thursday is named for the command that Christ gave His followers at the Last Supper to love one another (*mandatum* in Latin—see John 13:34). The name may refer to the Latin *mundo*, meaning "to wash," referring, of course, to Jesus washing

His disciples' feet. It has been seen as a day of reflection since the days of the early church.

In the Eastern church, Good Friday is actually called "Great Friday." This day is the commemoration of the ultimate sacrifice that Jesus paid on our behalf. It is a solemn day, punctuated by a corporate worship experience where the church comes together to celebrate the provision of redemption, and to remember the huge payment that was necessary to purchase it.

A popular monk in the Middle Ages sent an invitation to everyone in his parish, informing them that he would preach a special sermon that Good Friday evening titled "The Love of God." He asked them to be sure they arrived before the sun set. Complying with their priest, everyone in town was dutifully in their seats as the gray hues of dusk turned to the blackness of night. The monk sat still at the altar as darkness crept into the chapel amid impatient murmurings from the anticipating parishioners. Suddenly a single flame pierced the darkness as the monk lit a candle. He walked toward the towering crucifix at the front of the altar and shone the light on the nail-pierced feet of Jesus. He then raised the candle to the hole in the Savior's side, and by each of His punctured palms. Then, while on his tiptoes, the light illuminated the thorn-bloodied forehead of the King of kings. Returning to his seat, he sat down, blew out the candle, and left for home.

The powerful depiction of the love of God is dramatized in the image of His Son humbly hanging, bloodied, and passive. We celebrate Good Friday every year at our church. We commemorate Jesus, who sacrificed Himself, uttering His last words: "It is finished."

On Easter Sunday the traditional chorus "He Is Risen, He Is Risen Indeed," echoes throughout the Christian world as redeemed people stand up and celebrate the fact that their Lord is alive, active, all-powerful, and desperately interested in their lives and ministry. But another holy observance is known in some parts of the Christian world as Holy Saturday or simply the Sabbath. The Bible devotes only one verse to the day, and none of the four Gospel writers recorded any meaningful events that happened on that first Sabbath after the Crucifixion.

"But they rested on the Sabbath in obedience to the commandment" (Luke 23:56).

I once read a sermon that encouraged us to imagine the aftermath of the execution scene in the capital of Israel that day. If we were to walk around Jerusalem during that in-between time when the disciples were reeling, the Romans were forgetting, and the Jews were relieved, I wonder if it would seem like another average day. Walking toward Golgotha, we might run across a cleanup crew. Asking one of the men if he had seen Jesus crucified, he might respond bluntly, "I think so. The prisoners all start to look the same after a while."

"What were you thinking as you watched Him die?" we would prod.

He might look at us incredulously and say: "Hey, I've worked at hundreds of these things, and we're planning another one after the Sabbath. It is over. The guy even said so with His last words, 'It is finished.' If I were you, I'd just let it go."

Moving toward the garden where Jesus was laid, the tomb would have been quiet, Jesus' body bound up inside, rigid and lifeless. A hulking man with coarse hands might be seen leaning against a tree, shoulders rising and falling rhythmically from his sobbing. Less than forty-eight hours earlier, this man, Peter, had sworn he would never betray his Master, and thrice he had done so before the rooster crowed. "Peter, why are you weeping?" we ask.

"It is finished," he replies. "All my hopes and dreams, the vision of the kingdom, the dream worth dying for, it was all for naught."

Caiaphas the high priest walks past the crumpled, torn clothes in the corner of his room as he heads to breakfast. It was a bit melodramatic to tear his clothing in the Sanhedrin the night before, but the act made his point and won the argument. Jesus was gone, and the nuisance had been eliminated. It was finished, and he could enjoy the Sabbath in peace. Similar sentiments were surely felt on the hill in the palace of the Roman governor, Pontius Pilate. Maybe his wife was sleeping in this Saturday morning after a week of poor sleep resulting from her nightmares about the Galilean. Pilate is wondering if news of this troublemaker has made it to Rome. He is worried for his position and relieved to hear that the gentle man died quickly and has been laid in the tomb.

A simple man out for a lazy Sabbath walk comes across a carcass hanging from an olive tree. Thirty pieces of silver are scattered on the rocks below, and for Judas it is truly finished.

Mary, the mother of Jesus, sits at the wooden kitchen table made by the hands of her first son, hands she saw nailed to a cross the day before. Her husband died years earlier, and now she has lost her firstborn too. The pain of bringing Him into the world was excruciating, but it was nothing compared to the agony of watching Him leave it. *He was such a promising boy*, she thinks, *and now it is finished.*

I wonder if Barabbas got drunk on Friday night? Hours after his unexpected release, he found his friends and hit the bars. Stumbling through the deserted dirt streets, head pounding with each rooster crow, he thinks of the innocent man who died in his place. *I've killed before, I'll kill again, but that poor slob . . . it's over for Him.*

In a humble but spacious home in Bethany, a brother and his sisters sit in silence. Lazarus is struck by the irony of it all. Weeks earlier he was laid to rest in a tomb, and Jesus called him out alive. Now full of life, he grieves the death of the Life Giver. Martha, weeping quietly on the front step, is not the beehive of activity she normally is. Mary stands against the wall, looking toward Jerusalem. She is thinking of His feet, at which she sat, the feet she saw dripping with liquid love the day before. Simultaneously the trio whisper symphonically: "I can't believe it is finished."

They all heard Jesus' last words—"It is finished"—and they all misinterpreted them. To Barabbas, Pontius Pilate, Judas, and

Caiaphas, "it" meant that Jesus was finished, His life was over, His ideals and irritation would be buried with Him. To Peter, Mary, Lazarus, Martha, and Mary, it meant that their hope was finished. The beliefs they had left their former lives to support were a fading reality, and hope was gone.

But Jesus didn't mean either of these things. He meant that the work was finished. Colossians 2:13 offers one of the most concise descriptions of the finished work of Christ in Scripture. In this text, Paul explained the two great works that were finished on the cross. The work of forgiveness was finished, and the defeat of Satan was finished.

The Work of Forgiveness Was Finished

"When you were dead in your sins and in the uncircumcision of your sinful nature, God made you alive with Christ" (Col. 2:13).

Salvation is God's action on behalf of sinners while they are still sinners. We don't have to get all cleaned up to be saved. Jesus

> Those who know they are spiritually hungry are swift to find the bread of God. And when they see the cross, they are fast to say, "I'm sorry. Come, Holy Spirit, for my emptiness must have your fullness now."
>
> —Calvin Miller

reaches down into the mire we call home and drags us out, overpowering the gravelike suction that endeavors to keep us down.

Someone asked a question in our new member orientation class that took us by surprise. One of the participants asked how we would feel about a non-Christian man who was a cross-dresser attending our church. The leadership of some churches might pull the person aside, request that he dress "according to his gender" and then warmly welcome him to the church. This would protect our children from having to be exposed to aberrant behavior, and it would protect the church attendees from being distracted during the service. My response to the question is, "If we ask him to work through his sin issues before bowing his knee to Christ, are we going to do the same for the seekers who enter our church with alcohol problems, pornography addictions, loose lips, or judgmental hearts? Most likely we would say, 'No, Jesus loves them just the way they are, but He loves them too much to let them stay that way.'"

If that is true, would it not also apply to the cross-dresser or the homosexual couple? How would Jesus handle the situation? Jesus spent a good percentage of His life being criticized for spending time with the "wrong people," the people who obviously lived outside God's will. Jesus hung out with the outcasts of religious faith because He knew that salvation came to those who recognized their need for it.

The pious religious leaders of the day were oblivious to the reprehensible nature of their sin. The tax collectors, women of the night, lepers, eunuchs, and cripples were excluded from religious activity until Jesus "made them alive." We all were dead in our transgressions until Jesus made us alive. Once we became alive, we could recognize the sin, name it, learn to hate it, and grow out of it.

Colossians 2:13 continues: "He forgave us all our sins." The word translated *forgave* is *charizomai*, which comes from the ancient custom of canceling debts. If we were to receive a phone call today from MasterCard saying, "We know you have an outstanding credit card debt of more than fifteen thousand dollars. We have however, decided to cancel your debt. Listen as we push the delete button," we would experience the joy of forgiveness.

We read on in verse 14: "having canceled the written code . . ." The "written code" is *cheirographon*, a technical term used of a certificate of indebtedness written in one's own hand, a personal IOU. The verse continues: "with its regulations . . ." The word *regulations* is translated from the word *dogmasin*, from which we get *dogma* or *dogmatism*. It means an organized and arranged list of laws, or codes. ". . . that was against us and that stood opposed to us."

So, our personal IOU is a list of how we have fallen short in attempting to live up to the law that God has given us. It is the recognition of our condemnation that stems from a correct view of God's rules, and then recognizing our failure to live up to them. If we want to see what Christ did with this damning IOU, we can look back to verse 14, where Paul said that Christ *canceled* the written code. *Canceled* refers to an action describing the scraping of used papyrus sheets so they could be written on again. The first-century reader would have pictured her sins wiped away, erased, scraped into oblivion. "He took it away, nailing it to the cross" (v. 14).

The *titulus* was a tablet fixed over the crucified person's head on which his crimes were written. Paul is telling us that in Jesus' case, it was our sins, not His, that were inscribed. The debt we have incurred by our failure to live up to God's standard is "paid in full" (the literal meaning of the word translated "finished" in the gospel narrative). This means that no more work is necessary.

At one of our Good Friday services, we built a bridge across our platform with the middle section left out. There was a chasm with a flowing river between the two halves. Our drama team, pretending to be a team of hikers, "happened" across the unfinished bridge, and many turned back. But one stayed, convinced the map in his hand was true, and convinced that in his hand was the only way to the destination. As he sat on the bridge attempting to discern his next step, some workmen came and finished the bridge. One carried the middle section across his shoulders, and they pounded nails into each corner, securing it into place. The hiker cautiously crossed and resolutely continued toward his final resting place.

Jesus was the bridge. He built it as He hung on the cross. We don't need to build it; we simply need to cross it. Construction was completed that day, leading Jesus to say, "It is finished." Jesus built the bridge with the Cross. We cross the bridge by sheer faith.

I think I first really grasped grace in the office of a counselor. I had gone to him because of my own doubts about God's forgiveness. I was a seminary graduate, the theologically astute son of a great Christian couple. I had read Yancey, I had even preached a series on grace to our church, but I hadn't really owned it myself. "I don't think you really believe in grace," he said to me.

Reacting emotionally, I spewed my "grace résumé" all over him, telling him he was wrong.

He came back at me. "If you did believe in grace, you would believe that God has forgiven you. The fact that you refuse to forgive yourself means that you don't think He has forgiven you, which means you don't believe in grace." I started to listen. "True biblical forgiveness means that as soon as you commit a sin, it is as though it had never happened as far as God is concerned. Do you believe that?"

That day, I finally got it. If God had forgiven my debt, it was foolish for me to continue to carry it around. Living in grace means choosing to believe that forgiveness really took place two thousand years before I committed the sin.

The Defeat of Satan Was Finished

Paul continued: "And having disarmed . . ." (Col. 2:15). In a military context, *disarmed* is taken literally, but politically speaking, *disarmed* means "stripped." Clothing was a visibly distinguishable mark of an authority figure in the ancient world. An authority figure would have flowing robes commensurate with his position in society. When defeated or demoted, the first symbolic act of the conqueror was to take the official into the court and to strip him before all the people, removing the royal clothing—a degrading experience. To whom did Jesus actually do this when

He died on the cross? "The powers and authorities"—Satan and his brood—"he made a public spectacle of them, triumphing over them by the cross" (v. 15).

When a victor returned home from battle, he would ride through the streets welcoming the cheers of his people. At the back of the processional, in chains and stripped of their clothing, the captives were jeered at, humiliated, and shamed by the mocking throngs. At the cross, Jesus levied the mortal blow to the evil one and his minions. As Jesus lay quiet in the tomb that first Sabbath, He sent demons scurrying for cover. Satan, writhing in pain, licked his gushing wound and lashed out at anyone foolish enough to go near.

On the other end of the supernatural spectrum, heaven resounded with glorious praise. The gates were opened, and the first one to dance through was a common criminal from Palestine who was fortunate enough to have been crucified next to Jesus. The Father smiled, the angels sang, and all creation rejoiced in the finished work of Christ. The work and the worm were finished.

As far as the finished work of forgiveness is concerned, it is helpful to distinguish between the history of salvation and the order of salvation.

The history of salvation is comprised of Christ's once-and-for-all work. These are nonrepeatable actions that occurred in history and have lasting impact to this day. These events include the Incarnation, the Crucifixion, the Resurrection, the Ascension, and Pentecost.

The order of salvation speaks to the continuing application of Christ's work in our lives today. Christ completed the work of salvation, but the working out of that salvation continues in people's lives today as each person bows his or her knee to the Anointed One. The same "already but still happening" principle applies to Jesus' victory over Satan.

A missionary was terrified when returning home from work one day to discover a twenty-foot-long python in his living room. He summoned the village people, who came running with a rifle. They asked the missionary to wait outside and proceeded to put one well-placed bullet in the head of the massive serpent. The snake started to shake and throw its body around the room. The villagers ran outside and watched in horror as the snake shook the little house for almost fifteen minutes. Eventually everything was quiet in the house, and they ventured back in to discover all of the home's furniture completely destroyed. The snake was finished the moment it received the bullet. But even though it was all but dead, the death had to be waited out.

When Christ said, "It is finished," He meant that all the work had been done. The bullet had found the head of the serpent, and the forgiveness of sins was now available to anyone who desired it. That being said, the serpent continues to writhe in pain, destroying anything and anyone until the death finally arrives, and lost people continue to apply the blood to their sin-stained souls.

All this work was done on Good Friday. Then Saturday came and the disciples rested, and waited. In the timeline of faith, the church lives in the waiting room of Saturday. The disciples' struggle was due to the fact that they were living between what they thought they believed and what their senses told them was the truth. Jesus told them He was the Life, and then He died. This was obviously a confusing set of circumstances because reality was decidedly different from their expecta-tions. A friend of mine once taught me that the difference between expectations and reality is called disappointment. The disciples were disappointed that day. One way to deal with the disappointment of dashed expectations is to lower the expec-tations. Another is to see reality climb to meet or exceed what we expected. It is easy to believe that the disciples spent that Saturday lowering their expectations. "Perhaps He didn't mean all those things, but we'll take the principles that still apply and try to make something work."

In our day, Christians find themselves disappointed by life and angry that God hasn't lived up to their expectations. This may be because we have forgotten that we live in Saturday. Saturday represents the gap between faith and fulfillment. Saturday is the bridge between what we believe and what we will one day see at His appearing. The disciples had an advantage over us in that they physically spent three years with Jesus. We have an advantage over them in that we know Easter happened. But they had to live in Saturday until their eyes met Him again face-to-face. We also must live in a Saturday's wait until our eyes meet Him face-to-face.

We pick through the junkyard of life, weary vagabonds longing for but finding nothing. The empty wine bottle of satisfaction leaves us restless. In the words of English rocker Mick Jagger, "I can't get no satisfaction."

Reflecting on the day that Saturday became a reality, Patricia wrote:

> We don't like to wait. We wait in doctors' offices with a sick child, sighing, thumbing through magazines to alleviate the tedium of worry. We wait at stoplights, in the checkout lane of grocery stores, in carpool lines, and in traffic jams, idling on the interstate an hour and a half before we're due at work. Waiting is something we want to pay others to do on our behalf, so we eat out and let the wait-staff cater to us. We don't want more time, but for time to pass and be quick about it.

Patricia experienced those insufferable nights of painful longing after the funeral guests had disappeared and the phone calls had steadied into a daily, monotonous rhythm:

> Time became an enemy to me because I had to live within its bounds, wounded to the soul. I went from desperately clawing to regain the day that had changed everything, to wanting to run from it, placing as much space between myself and that hateful hour as possible. But time passed no more swiftly in May or June than it had in April.

I came to realize that I wasn't running away from April 27, but running to something I could not see. I had been handed a new set of marching orders for my life that whipped me around and gave me strange new bearings.

I no longer sat making goals for myself and teaching my children to do the same. I had seen the end of a driven life, and mine was futile. The goals and mandates I had passed along to my college-age daughter were frivolous—keep a high grade point average, lead the pack, and outdo the competition did not help Jessi cross the road more carefully. What carried her forth in her last few minutes here in the waiting room was a simple dictum I had taught her in the midst of all our other busyness—trust Jesus for everything.

While the helicopter roared toward the hospital to save her, she was engaged in crossing an uncommon road. Celestial greetings from another world met her to take her on the remaining leg of her journey. She had been taught to trust Jesus for everything. Now she could trust Him to walk her the rest of the way home.

In the words of our precious friend Randy Alcorn, Jessi was finally home.

Now I wait. My life has been retooled. Education is not a device to help my son "get ahead," but a learning experience to enjoy, to feast upon! We take walks, eat meals together, play Scrabble in the evenings, make less money, and enjoy our life here together in the waiting room.

When we stumble upon a hurting life, we do not step over and hurry on our way, but bend down to ask what we can do to help.

The minutes do not tick past any faster or slower when I'm using up my time in selfish pursuit than when I'm taking a moment to encourage a friend or explain an algebra problem to my son. Either way, time passes. How I use the minutes here in the Saturday of my journey will either leave a stamp of permanence upon a human heart or blow away like dust. Saturday is the place where we learn abiding trust. It is the only justifiable tool we need to cross the road.

Saturday is the embodiment of our faith. We wait by faith for Jesus to return or for Him to take us home, trusting that Easter will become a firsthand reality for us. While we wait, we feel

> What's wrong with being number two?
>
> **—Morrie Schwartz**

the repercussions of a vindictive evil presence that desires to harm us, mislead us, and discourage us, flailing about our lives like a dictator that won't admit he's whipped. This is the world in which we live. But while Saturday is where we live, Sunday is coming.

So, when we lose our jobs, our children get ill, our bodies fall apart, our relationships suffer, and our portfolios vanish, we have a choice. We can become frustrated and disappointed, or we can remember that we live in the Sabbath, the "in-between time," after the work of salvation has been accomplished in our hearts and before we rise again to new life in the heavenlies. We can remember that Satan is wounded and wicked, and we can focus our hearts and minds on the sabbath rest God has promised us in Hebrews 4.

When Winston Churchill planned his funeral service, he ended it with two solos played back-to-back on trumpet. The first solo, "Taps," customarily honored a fallen countryman. After a brief pause, the trumpeter played "Reveille," the upbeat celebratory piece that is the antithesis of "Taps." Churchill wanted the attendees of his funeral to feel the difference between the sadness of Good Friday—"Taps"—and the joy of Easter—"Reveille." The short pause in between represented the Saturday in which we live. It is short, it will pass, and while we dwell here we would be wise to remember the one thing we *know* the disciples remembered that day: "But they rested on the Sabbath in obedience to the commandment" (Luke 23:56).

While we labor in an uncertain waiting room this side of heaven, we can take a well-needed sabbath rest knowing that it is a period of reflection on the time the earth stood paralyzed outside a quiet tomb, awaiting a verdict. Whether we take this time of reflection on Saturday, or Sunday, or any weekday, we know that the real meaning of the Sabbath rest was quietly explosive—a day when evil met its match, chains dropped from our souls, and blinders fell from our eyes.

Like silent thunder.

No wonder God calls it holy.

Turned-Over Leaves

Self-denial begets character and character servanthood. But just giving up "stuff" we enjoy will not bring us to a sterling humanity.

—CALVIN MILLER

We all have love/hate relationships. My primary love/hate relationship is with golf. Another is with any form of discipline—loving what it does for me, but hating to apply myself to it.

October 1, my alarm woke me a little before 6:00 A.M. and I stumbled into my closet. I put on my swimsuit, my sweatshirt, grabbed a water bottle out of the fridge, and hopped into my car. The chill of morning was already weakening my resolve as I drove to the outdoor pool where I swim laps in the morning. Punching in the member's pass code, I gazed over the dark water and thought to myself, *Why am I here?* Having already put on my cap, my lap counter was safely secured to my index finger. The cool fall breeze rippled the pool's surface. My rule that says once I touch the water I have to jump in before I count to five, left me lingering on the bank.

After a moment of assessment, I reconsidered my exercise of choice. A month earlier, frustrated with my lack of physical exercise, I had "turned over a new leaf." I had chosen swimming because my bad back doesn't allow me to play basketball anymore. Swimming is great for sore joints, and it combines muscle training and cardio at the same time. But standing on the bank with no one to urge me into the water, those logical thoughts didn't carry much weight.

"As I study people like Merton, Benedict, Francis of Assisi, John Wesley, Charles de Foucauld, Mother Teresa," said Philip Yancey, "I see in these disciplined souls not set-jaw determination but rather spontaneity and even joy. By investing their freedom in discipline, they secure a deeper freedom unavailable elsewhere . . . St. Benedict counseled the need for 'a little strictness in order to amend faults and guard love,' and perhaps that formula provides the guideline to keep disciplines from tilting to the extremes."[1] Yancey explains in his study of the Benedictine order that the rule of Benedict is more wisdom than law: "The Rule of Benedict is a way of life. And that's the key to understanding the Rule. It isn't one."[2]

Wisdom provides the undercurrent to our resolve—the *why* to our *why nots*. If we are to live life beyond the self's demanding inventory, we have need of the right criterion, one rich in life-giving pronouncements, pulsing with altruistic pursuits that return to the self its fuel for the journey. If all we have are jaw-clenching new rules, we have traded the gold for the dross. We have learned nothing new, trading maturity for temporary fixes.

During my annual review, Burton French, the chairman of our elder board, asked me: "Pete, what was the biggest lesson that God taught you this last year?" It was not a profound lesson. For me to paint the picture, I've got to take you back about a year and a half to a sermon I preached after my sabbatical. The church kindly granted my family and me two months to go and rest. Before returning home renewed and with some new resolve, Libby and I decided: *It's going to be different when we get home.* We decided we were going to incorporate this lesson of sabbath rest, of being still and quiet. We could finally hear God's still and quiet voice, and we never wanted to lose what we had found. We decided we would do it often enough to connect with Him in a personal and intimate way on a consistent basis.

We *turned over a new leaf* when we got back, but then found ourselves sliding right back into the old habits. In America, we turn over new leaves all the time. This phenomenon usually raises its head around January 1. "This year will be different," we say. "I'm going to have a quiet time every day this year. I'm going to exercise five times a week. I'm going to be nice to my brother. I'm going to give 10 percent to my church. I'll even choke down Aunt Mildred's fruitcake next Christmas without complaining."

By the time Cupid's cards are being sold at the local drug-store, 95 percent of our leaves have been returned to their pre-turned posture. Now even the fate of Aunt Mildred's fruitcake hangs in the balance.

Jesus never turned over *new leaves*; instead, He established new *norms*. "He who was seated on the throne said, 'I am making everything new!' Then he said, 'Write this down, for these words are trustworthy and true'" (Rev. 21:5). Jesus is saying to us, "I am making everything new," and then He looked at John and said, "Make sure you write that down! This is trustworthy; this is true. I want everybody to hear this. I am making everything new."

If you read the book of Revelation, you'll see the New Jerusalem, the new heavens, the new earth, the new wine, the new stone, and the new name. But the new things do not arrive at the end of time. Jesus has been making things new from the beginning. More accurately, Jesus has been establishing newness since the beginning of time.

When we use the word *new*, we tend to think of something that is beginning, something that wasn't here yesterday but is here now. That is one aspect of newness in Scripture, but it's not the whole picture. Two words in the original language of the New Testament show us a complete definition. *Neos* means "new" and "what was not there before." So if we plant a new tree in our yard, a neighbor might notice and say: "Hey, that's a new tree that wasn't there yesterday." It is *neos*. Not here until now. Another aspect of newness in Scripture is described for us in the Greek word *kainos*—a much deeper, richer word than *neos*. It means what is new and distinctive, new in nature, different from the usual, superior in value, permanent, and established. *Neos* is a *new leaf. Kainos* is a new paradigm.

The Kainos Work of Jesus

In Luke 22:20 we see the *kainos covenant*—the new covenant: "In the same way, after the supper, [Jesus] took the cup, saying, 'This cup is the new covenant [the *kainos* covenant] in my blood, which is poured out for you.'"

Picture Jesus coming to us and saying, "All right, folks, we've decided to make a change. We're going back to the Davidic covenant. No more salvation through the blood, and no more forgiveness of sins. We're going back to the old ways of when David was king. This means if you are in the line of David, you might be in luck. Otherwise, you're tough out of luck." This isn't going to happen.

Jesus established the new covenant, one that lasts forever, new in quality, superior in value, permanent, and established. The new covenant is two thousand years old. An "old new" *Kainos* goes on because Jesus does not take us back to the old way.

Another example is the *kainos command* in John 13:34: "A new command I give you: Love one another. As I have loved you, so you must love one another." The newness of that command is not to love one another. God had been telling the people of Israel to do that for centuries. The newness of the command is to love *as I have loved you.* Jesus introduced a new kind of love, a selfless love that any follower of His must emulate—love that issues from our hearts through our lives, our gifts, and even our trials. Loving as He loved takes a moment of reflection where we turn the scope away from ourselves to see how others live, and then respond.

We have the *kainos life:* "Just as Christ was raised from the dead through the glory of the Father, we too may live a new life" (Rom. 6:4). It's not just that it is different from the way it was yesterday, but it is new, established, and permanent until the day that Jesus comes back. Eternal. My new life is now thirty-four years and counting.

Jesus has provided for us the *kainos way:* "But now, by dying to what once bound us, we have been released from the law so that we serve in the new way of the Spirit, and not in the old way of the written code" (Rom. 7:6).

Will Jesus ever say, "I realize you've grown accustomed to grace, but we're going back to law. I want you to start in Leviticus. Go ahead and get started on that as soon as you can. Each week we'll be doing an evaluation on you based on the Ten Commandments. I'll be conducting it. If you fail . . . well, we'll burn that bridge when we get to it"?

Fortunately, we never have to return to the old law's yoke. Jesus established a new code designed with wings of grace. He is never going to go back or change His mind. He is never going to flip the leaf over. *Kainos.* New.

With His *kainos* code, we have the freedom to work and then the permission to take our rest in Him. He gave it to us for our benefit, yet we struggle to make it "work" for us. We get caught up in the hectic stratum of living, and then feel as though lying down is like dropping into a well from which we will never climb out.

"Sometimes I get so busy I find myself making comments like, 'I wish I didn't have to sleep.' Yet God is so wise, for if He hadn't given our bodies this *need*, we'd fill the extra time with more busyness," said Christian novelist Nancy Moser. She has found that her time of rest is at specific times in her work-at-home day:

> I've found that the best way to use my time wisely—and find time to really enjoy rest—is to recognize my best times of day. I am a morning person and do my creative work starting at 4:30 or 5:00 A.M. By noon my brain is shot creatively, so I use the rest of the day and evening for less mind-bending projects. By not trying to cater to all types of to-do lists at all times of the day, but knowing when they fit best into my very specific mental and physical capabilities, I can rest easier and more completely at night.

Moser is not living out a new set of rules, but applying wisdom to natural physical functions. She has found a working life lived out by the Spirit, the freedom of life yoked to the Spirit. She is not touting a formula for others to follow, except the one that follows God's leading.

The *kainos creation* in 2 Corinthians 5:16 begins: "So from now on," the virtual battle cry of the new covenant. "From now on we regard no one from a worldly point of view. Though we once regarded Christ in this way, we do so no longer. Therefore, if anyone is in Christ, he [or she] is a new creation; the old has gone, the new has come!" (vv. 16–17). The *kainos* has come.

Once a new creation—always a new creation. Jesus will never ask us to go back to the lives of bitterness, doubt, jealousy, and rage that we once used to live. The bondage to sin and to addictions, the loneliness, hopelessness, and lostness—we never have to go back to that old creation. Once a new creation—always a new creation. Jesus didn't turn over new leaves.

Biblically Driven and Spiritually Sustained

A new normal for our lives in the Spirit is a fundamental shift in the way we do life that lasts for the rest of our lives. By definition it should be two things. It should first of all be *biblically driven*. I was reading Scripture recently and came across something that Jesus wanted me to be as His disciple. Scripture is a depository of kainos expectations. Here is one: "Love the Lord your God with your heart, soul, mind, and strength"(see Mark 12:30). Now that you are a disciple of Jesus Christ, you will love Him with all of your heart, you will love Him with all of your soul, you will love Him with all of your mind, and you will love Him with all of your strength. To love Him with all of your mind means different things, depending on mental ability, mental capacity, and mental interest. Jesus expects me to live and love this way, from now on.

Second, our life in Christ should be *spiritually sustained*. This new way of life is in the Holy Spirit, not by the law. This isn't a list of rules, but avenues by which the Holy Spirit can create in us Christlikeness. Instead of making a rigid affirmation, quoting mantras like "I can change, I can change," we can submit to the Spirit's higher work and admit, "Oh, Lord Jesus, You need to do this through me." Birthed of the Spirit, our lives will find a higher success ratio. The old normal is jealous, powerful, and ruthless. It requires no effort to sustain because it is the embodiment of human status quo. The old life, like a bad neighborhood, is self-sustaining unless, by the power of the Spirit, we move away to the newer, better neighborhood.

Life often lives us instead of the other way around. Do you remember in the westerns when the horse-drawn stage coach, lacking a driver, was careening towards the precipice while Johnny Hero climbed across the horses' backs to the cheers of the distressed damsel inside? Do you feel the frantic pace, the helpless lack of control, the impending doom? That is how I felt when I wrote me letter to Burton. I was no longer living my life, my life was living me! Far beyond a mere academic exercise, my personal struggle led to desperation. I sat and penned this letter to the chairman of our elder board:

Good morning, Burton.

Libby and I have had a couple of really healthy discussions lately and I've made some decisions that I'd like to communicate to you, discuss, receive your blessings, and move forward on. First of all, I think I need to say that Libby and I are in a bit of trouble. Our marriage is sound and the kids are healthy and doing well, and these are obvious gifts of God's grace. However, if we were to continue to live life as we now do, I think it is fair to say that we would not be able to sustain our ministry at Bent Tree. Seeing that my goal is long-term effective ministry and maintaining a fundamental desire to prioritize my marriage and raise my kids well, I need to make some somewhat drastic changes in my work life. Allow me to define the word *trouble* a little more precisely: (1) I'm not discipling and providing the attention my kids need. (2) I'm not nurturing and caring for Libby the way I need to. (3) I'm not feeding myself spiritually or intellectually the way I need to. (4) I'm not developing the leaders of the church the way I need to. (5) I'm not caring for the elders the way I need to. (6) I'm not investing the time I need into my sermons.

Burton, you may find yourself asking, "Well then what in the world is he doing?" Please listen to my answer to this rhetorical question. The simple answer to that is: *I'm doing what everyone else wants me to do.* As a result, I'm failing at my key responsibilities. My ministerial life is extremely intense, and I have no margin or time to nurture my own spiritual walk. The result is a dryness and a lessening in passion for the ministry.

My cry for help was well received. My attempt to define and describe what the old life looks like as far as sabbath rest and health are concerned for me was now something I could conquer. To throw out the old normal, we need to be honest, sitting down to delineate the facts of our lives. Then we need to ask God how He wants us to live so that we can introduce sabbath rest and quiet into our lives.

A number of years ago, teacher, author, and pastoral trainer Ramesh Richard told the story of a professor standing in front of the class with a big glass jar, attempting to teach time management skills. He filled it with big rocks and asked, "Is this jar filled?"

The students said, "Yes, it's full."

He took out a bag of pebbles and filled it up and asked them again, "Now is it full?"

"Oh, sure. Now it's full," they answered.

The professor took out a bag of sand and filled the jar. The sand filled in the spaces among all the pebbles and the big rocks.

He asked, "Now is it full?"

They looked at it and agreed it was full. Then he took a big pitcher of water and filled up the jar so it was overflowing. When he asked again if the jar was full, the students were then fearful of being tricked again. They answered, "No, no, it's not full."

He said, "Yes. Now it's full. Nothing else is going into the jar." Then he asked, "What is the lesson of this demonstration?"

One student raised her hand and said, "The lesson is that you can always squeeze more things into your schedule if you try really hard." The professor explained why she was wrong. The example of the jar is: *If you don't put the big rocks in first, you'll never get them in.*

Like the jar, our lives are so full of water, sand, and pebbles that we leave no space in our lives for the big rocks. In my letter to Burton, I listed six of my big priorities, the things that I should have placed first in the jar of my life. Those are my big rocks, yet they weren't incorporated into my life. Instead, my life was full of pebbles and sand—the things that others expected of me. While important, they are not the big rocks. With the *old normal*, our lives are so full that there's no time for God. Living out a life that is patterned to please God offers me peace and intimacy with my Savior and those whom I love.

We face the challenge of the four quadrants in our lives. Steven Covey's book *Seven Habits of Highly Effective People* impressed me so much that I have taught its principles in classes a half dozen times. But it has taken time to incorporate the principles into my own life. I am now starting to finally live these principles. Just as a little fertilizer takes time to produce better tomatoes, new principles take time to bring change into our lives. Covey says that there are four quadrants in life.

Quadrant 1: Important and Urgent

These are our daily work responsibilities, those things outlined in our job descriptions that must be done today. They fall under the tyranny of the important, urgent. We accomplish these tasks most of the time. To keep our families in the manner to which they are accustomed, we must fulfill these daily obligations.

Quadrant 2: Important but Not Urgent

In a Christian's life, these duties may include spending time with God and investing time in His Word and prayer. Important to us, but not urgent. We can survive this day without having had a quiet time. Physical exercise is something that we believe is important because we've heard its benefits taught our entire lives. Yet we do not consider it urgent. If we put it off, no one knows but us. Spending time with our families is another duty that is important yet not urgent. Lying in the grass with our kids, looking up at the clouds and deciding which one looks like a bunny are important moments. Yet we can go three whole years without doing it, and no one would notice.

Quadrant 3: Urgent but Not Important

These are duties that are not important to us, but they are usually important to someone else. Thus they get laid on our plate. We are informed that they should be urgent, but we don't share that same sense of urgency with the bearer of the task.

Quadrant 4: Not Important and Not Urgent

Junk mail, e-mail jokes, and shuffling papers are time wasters handed to us by those who fail to understand that we have no room in the jar for such things. And then there are the other rocks that are shoved into our jar, such as attending "waste-of-time" meetings where a novice leader called a meeting because it was expected of her. A pastor on the staff of a large church once complained about the forced attendance at such meetings where the new minister was trying to prove his unseasoned leadership abilities by calling the staff together for frequent and aimless chat sessions. One day the dialogue droned on to the point that the staff pastor, desperate to get back to the work waiting for him, stood up in his chair and shouted, "Someone stop him or I'll jump!"

These are the rocks that we do not ask for, yet there they are, taking up space in our lives. Our biggest problem rests between Quadrant 2 and Quadrant 3. Our lives fill up with Quadrant 3 and we never get around to Quadrant 2. Our time usage will be both effective and efficient by ensuring that Quadrant 2 activities fill our calendars first.

We face the challenge of *the tyranny of the yes* versus *the tenacity to the mission.* When our church was small, I would always get frustrated with the pastors of large churches because they seemed to become less and less accessible as their churches got bigger and bigger. I made myself a promise that such a practice would never be mine. I would be fully accessible to everybody 100 percent of the time.

Bent Tree Bible Fellowship now has grown substantially, and it was taking me up to four hours to reply to e-mails when my e-mail address was fully accessible to everyone. One day I took a step back and asked myself, *Why are you doing this?* I knew the answer: I did not want anyone to perceive me as being inaccessible. But to pastor the church effectively, I had to assess the big rocks first. Delegating this task was a difficult change for me. But it bought me three to four more hours a day to invest in the big rocks. Whatever we say yes to causes our lives to fill up, squeezing out the most important things. Tenacity to the mission teaches us to say either, "I can't" or, "Is there someone else who could handle this for us?" To do this well, of course, we have to understand our mission.

Many Christian authors were finding that the more popular their books became, the more requests they were receiving to speak at book clubs, school book fairs, and all sorts of events that had nothing to do with their earliest mission. This problem was discussed among their peers, and one author spoke up and told them that she had learned to define her mission in a statement.

She printed it off and kept it above her workstation. Whenever she received a request to speak, she would study her mission statement. If the event did not fit within the framework of her mission, she kindly declined the offer. All of these writers adopted the same philosophy and renewed their resolve to focus on the written word that God had given them for their life's work.

God has a life's work for each of us. When we take the time to define our missions, we begin to understand our boundaries, just like a missionary who is assigned to a particular village. When we understand our missions, we are better equipped to minister effectively to our "villages." My life mission statement is twofold: to serve my bride and our children, and to serve the bride of Christ and her children. This gives me a framework from which I can make choices.

We can take time to sift for the best instead of settling for the great. One of the things our family desired is that we spend more evenings at home to have a family sabbath, so that our rest could be a mutual enjoyment. One of our goals was to try to have at least three evenings a week at home. Because of a full calendar, some time had to pass before we found a week with three open nights. A good friend called during our first evening off, one with whom we loved to fellowship. He said, "Pete, I've got a luxury box all to ourselves tonight for the Dallas Stars game. Can you and Libby come?" Turning him down was painful.

Later in the week, we got a call from some friends who invited us to join them for a gathering of several friends. As I held the phone against my cheek, Libby looked at me and said, "Are we going to do this new normal or not?" My new normal requires that I sift through the great things and choose the best. Those two nights that we stayed home were chilly outside. We made a fire, sat around with the kids, and we read a Christmas story to them. I remember my heart so full of rest and joy, I thought: *It doesn't get any better than this*. We chose the best instead of what seemed good.

Patricia Hickman and her husband, Randy, were frustrated at having so little family time when Randy was at Bible school all day and working on many evenings. So she and Randy sat down and decided that the reason they were so exhausted was that they spent their downtime watching late-night television together. They decided that until he graduated, they would get rid of all television. Their children loved their family time so much that the parents left the cable off for seven years. The youngest child grew up having had no television at all, and when asked at Christmas what he wanted, always said, "I don't know what you mean. I have everything I need." Without the commercialism of television, materialism disappeared from this family's life. It all started by focusing on family time together in the evenings in order to enjoy a sabbath rest.

We can compare unreachable goals to reachable characteristics. When we turn over new leaves, we usually set aligned goals. When we establish new normals, we reach for abiding character. Herein is our struggle: what we intend to do. We set goals such as, "I'm going to have a quiet time every day this year and spend time studying spiritually enriching books." Two different results may arise with such a goal. The first result is that I might reach it. The second result is that I might not.

We reach the year's end and then mentally check off that last box on December 31. As we embrace a sense of triumph, we neglect to ask: What did I study this year? How did God speak to me in His Word this year? We check off our goals but can't recollect a single connection with God. Or else we reach March 1 and then miss a day. After missing one day, we feel we can't reach our goal. So we miss another day, a week, and eventually give up altogether. Goals are terrible that way. *We need to look behind the goals to the characteristics they are designed to create.* We want to experience growth in our lives. We consider the goal of having a quiet time every day as a bridge to that growth. But what is more important is the something that we desire. That is our new normal.

When we prioritize our big rocks first and then aim for things that reshape our character instead of our image to others, we can say: "I intend from now on, in the power of the Spirit, to be characterized by . . . ," and then seek out the spiritually driven motives. Turning over a new leaf proclaims, "I'm going to have a quiet time every day." Instead, we can say, "I intend from now on, by the power of the Spirit, to be characterized by being a man of God's Word or a woman of God's Word." From this day until the day we die, we can be characterized as having a passion for God's Word.

Our avenue for reaching a spiritually driven life will come to us as we place the big rocks first into our lives. This is not some new discovery, but the simple plan that God has already laid out for us. That is why it works.

Other new proclamations can be anything from "I intend from now on, in the power of the Spirit, to be characterized by eating in a healthy manner" as opposed to "I'm going to lose eight pounds this year." In other words, I'm simply going to be characterized as a person who takes care of the temple. That means I can have a big juicy burger and fries every once in a while and not feel guilty because eating healthy and taking care of myself physically characterizes me. What is important is how my life characterizes Christ, who lives in me. How does my life look from this day forth?

In addition to our spiritual and physical lives, we also must consider our emotional lives. Perhaps you've heard the old tapes that you play inside your head, the things that people said to you over the years, things that perhaps you did not believe yet caused you to live your life according to those old tapes. But when we give our emotions a sabbath rest we can say, "I intend from now on, in the power of the Spirit, to be characterized by listening to what God says about me."

In keeping with this new paradigm, we may adopt the avenue of spending this year memorizing Ephesians 1 in order to train up our emotions in a new self-image. Our old normal challenges us to invest time in television, movies, sports, games, or computer work, instead of investing time in reading. We can say, "I intend from now on, in the power of the Spirit, to be characterized by reading books that will challenge me intellectually and enable me to grow in my love for Him."

The old way says that the family gets our leftovers. The new normal says, "I intend, in the power of the Spirit, to be characterized by discipling my kids." Before, we assumed that our marriages would be strong without much input from either spouse. The new normal says, "I intend from now on, in the power of the Spirit, to be characterized by connecting on a consistent basis with my spouse." That may be a weekly date night or a monthly date night with our aim being consistency.

We can apply God's new normal to every area of our lives, even to stewardship. We used to think, "I will give minimally when I have some left over." But from now on we intend, in the power of the Spirit, to be characterized by honoring God first with our money."

We can study God's Word and come up with amounts and percentages; we can accomplish a diligence to the big rocks in regard to our work, the ministry, or any aspect of our lives. The profundity is not in the idea or the lesson. The profundity is in the application of it.

Here a simple table provides a matrix of change.

Old Life	New Life
Small rocks first	Big rocks first
Quadrant 3	Quadrant 2
Tyranny of the "yes"	Tenacity of the moment (or mission)
Settling for the great	Sifting for the best
Unreachable goals	Reachable characteristics

When Jesus came to Earth and handed us His opportunity for a new normal, He did not lay it on top of the old ways telling us to get busy piecing both together. Instead, He promised that His yoke would be something that we could carry because He would be sharing the load. He brought us a new covenant and with two arms extended, He wiped the desktop clean of all the old clutter. Since then, we have been busy adding the old ways back on top of the new. Old habits die hard.

I jumped into the water that fall morning. I do not want a new leaf. A cared-for life requires making the hard choices. The water was frigid. I literally screamed out loud when I came up for my first breath of air, but a few laps later I was completely acclimated to the temperature. Forty minutes later I sat down in my car, warm again, loving discipline and its benefits.

When I apply the same discipline to my life that includes stopping my work, resting, and reflecting on my life in the Spirit, I love the profits passed on to both body and soul. Our very nature thrives on and is nurtured by stillness, solitude, and discipline. The soul of man is a mysterious, invisible core, needing to connect with its own Creator, yet lacking the know-how to hear into the spiritual realm. It is when we lay our heads in the Father's lap, close our eyes and listen, that we hear the music that will bring us rest.

That is how we learn that we can finally throw away the turned-over leaves we have sewn together to cover up our flaws and nakedness. With Christ as our new covering, we are handed the wisdom we need to live a life of new normalcy.

A Plan for Your Sabbath Rest

Life is not a problem to be solved but a work to be made,
and that work may well utilize much raw material that we
would prefer to do without.

—PHILIP YANCEY

And God who gives beginning gives the end . . . A rest for
broken things too broke to mend.

—JOHN MANSFIELD

Long before my sabbatical frolicking with the loons on Spider Lake, my future wife waded into the same waters. She was a teenager at summer camp. Earlier that day, she had made a decision to obey the Lord by being baptized. *This day,* she thought to herself, *is the day I stake my claim, the day I make my parents' faith my own.* Ron, her favorite camp counselor, was going to be doing the baptism, and she eagerly anticipated Ron dunking her. She retold the story to our children years later around the dinner table. "I made the decision that even if my parents were to turn their backs on Christ and tell me Christianity was a joke, I would still follow Him."

She excitedly told her friends about the baptism in the lake, asked them to come and, procuring their commitment to do so, eagerly anticipated the sacred time. Early that afternoon, as she walked toward the water, she saw her friends heading the opposite direction. On their way to the snack shop, they didn't turn back when seeing her. As she walked into the water, she got in the "wrong line" and suddenly there was another man, whom she didn't know, preparing to baptize her while Ron stood a few feet away with another youth. Floods of disappointment swept over her. Her family wasn't there, her friends didn't bother to show up, Ron wasn't baptizing her—everything was going wrong. She felt very alone.

Then the still, small voice of the Holy Spirit whispered to her tender soul, "Libby, following Jesus is about standing alone for Him. You just told Me this morning that you were determined to follow Jesus whether others did or not. Well, here you are, alone with Jesus." She walked out of the water a different person that day. Her faith was truly her own, and she was willing to stand alone.

In order to claim the life we long to live, we have to make similar commitments. Sometimes we stand alone in our values. In fact, everyone else will make life harder for us. As with any change we want to bring to our lifestyle, starting out with someone else's plan can frustrate us, like riding someone else's bicycle without adjusting the seat. So as each of us work out a planned rest, we have to plan the best time and organize the available human resources to fill in during our absence. We may need to use a portion of our vacation time or take days off without pay. Or we may simply plan our sabbath rest around our normal days off.

A long-term sabbatical is a rare gift that many organizations or families cannot afford to offer. If you find yourself in a place where a break of a month or two is possible, there are preparations necessary before you go. First of all, make sure you have exhibited a work ethic that predisposes your church or company toward giving you time off. Some of us work alongside coworkers who think they work harder than other people. Before asking for time off, take some time to analyze your work ethic. Have you earned your paycheck? Simply stated, do you deserve a sabbatical? If, in all honesty, you conclude your effort and value to the group you serve has warranted a sabbatical, I would encourage you to follow these steps:

- Speak to a trusted leader in your organization and ask if there is a policy concerning sabbaticals. If so, follow the policy, if not . . .

- Share your desire to take an elongated break with rationale from your personal life and any lessons you have learned in this book.

- Ask your employer to read *Secrets from the Treadmill* and then meet to discuss it.

- Plan your sabbatical with goals and action steps and write a proposal for your decision-making body. Include how you will cover your responsibilities when you are gone. Include in your proposal all the details necessary to answer questions before they are asked. For example: Is there a sabbatical allowance? Is vacation time affected in any way by this sabbatical? (When I took my two-month break, I gave back two weeks of vacation that year. As a result of my new normal, I am now out of the office the full month of July every year. However, those weeks are comprised of vacation, study leave, and ministry leave weeks that I had already been granted.)

- Should a policy be written to govern potential future requests from other staff members?

- Enter into discussions with them with an open heart. Realize they have the right to say no, and if they decline your request, accept that decision with grace.

- If they say yes, make sure you respond with gratitude at least once before you leave. Send to them a thorough summary of your time away upon your return.

Let me take you back to Spider Lake one more time. I was a junior-high pastor, and Truman Robinson, the founder of Fort Wilderness camp, was taking us on a hike and campout. It was hot and sticky, the hike was fairly long, and I was responsible for 150 junior-high students. We set up camp near the lake and settled down for a good night's rest; at least we adults had settled upon the idea.

The heat was stifling—then the mosquitoes decided to have a convention on the same site we had chosen. I imagined the clarion call going out over all of northern Wisconsin, "Two hundred hot, sweaty people to suck dry over by Spider Lake!" The mosquitoes flew in from all over the world.

By the time the embers had cooled to a warm pulse, the kids were screaming, and I had buried my head in my sleeping bag. The problem being, of course, that it was about 120 degrees inside my sleeping bag, so I periodically had to come up for air. Each time I did, I let another fifty or so of those blood-sucking bugs into my bag. I invested the next twenty minutes attempting to kill them, creating more heat, and so the cycle continued. The only up side to the situation was that inside my bag I couldn't hear the wails of my kids.

I did hear Truman laughing in his sleeping bag. "In fifty years of sleeping under the stars, I've never seen this many mosquitoes in one place!" he chortled. By all accounts it is fair to say that rest was impossible that night. But the most amazing thing happened. Eventually, we all fell asleep.

When we woke up the next morning, we all had hundreds of bumps. But we had rested. You may think it is impossible to find rest in our crazy world, but it isn't. You might have to sacrifice some of your comforts, and you may have some bumps to show for it, but God is capable of giving you sabbath rest amid the most challenging life circumstances.

The majority of people reading this book will simply never have an opportunity to take a long break. But sabbath rest is certainly not out of reach. You may take a full day once a quarter and work out with your spouse child-care responsibilities so that he or she can take a day too. You may pause on your train ride to work. You may settle in for a time of personal worship in the evening after the kids have gone to bed. It could be as fleeting as a ten-minute silent pause in your car before going inside to your workplace. As your plan for a sabbath rest is shaped, it can be as simple as taking a day of seclusion in a park with a journal.

But What Will I Do?

The thought of taking a full day alone in a park might cause some of you to laugh out loud. *What in the world will I do with all that time?* we think. In actuality, it is stunning how quickly a day passes. I would encourage you to start by asking yourself what type of sabbath rest you need. Ask yourself the following questions and put an X next to the one that resonates with you.

1. Do I need to deepen my walk with Christ?
2. Do I need to find answers to spiritual questions, doubts, or ask God if a new direction is needed in my life?
3. Do I need to relieve the stress and the feeling of being under my life instead of on top of it?
4. Do I need to study a particular book of the Bible and see how it applies to my own life (or some other meaningful book of life applications)?
5. Do I need to build trust between God and myself?
6. Do I need to analyze where I am in my life and decide why I feel stagnant in my work, my home life, or in my church work?
7. Do I need to seek a Christ-honoring time in nature and to find God in the big picture of His creation?
8. Do I need to deal with inward pain such as depression or grief and then decide if I should seek counsel?
9. Do I need to spend time deciding how I can simplify my life and search my priorities?

10. Other reasons I need to seek a rest:

_____

_____

After determining the hopes for the day, you can plan it out. By getting away with nothing but our Bibles, we can focus our time on holy leisure—focusing minutes on nothing but God. We can also read a children's book, a good novel, take a hike in nature—anything that calms us and brings our thoughts to a halt and into a meditative, reflective state. By working through the following checklist, your planning will bear fruit.

My Personal Plan for a Recharged Heart

First Steps:

My plan for finding a responsible replacement: _____

_____

_____

Minding the home front: My plan for caring for my family while I recharge my life:

_____

_____

_____

My place of retreat:

_____

My budget for my retreat: _____

(Some retreats offer scholarships to certain groups such as pastors, pastors' wives, artists, or writers. Or if your family can help with your children, you can turn your own home into a retreat.)

My personal goals for recharging my life:

1. _____ (What will a recharged life do for me spiritually?)
2. _____ (What will a recharged life do for me when I return to work?)
3. _____ (How will a recharged life improve my relationships?)
4. _____ (What will a recharged life do for me as God's disciple?)
5. _____ (What do I hope to learn?)

My commitment to leaving behind unnecessary distractions:
I leave behind the following things/distractions that interrupt my quiet time with God:

_____

I leave behind the following attitudes that hinder my time of renewal:

_____

The Journey of Silent Listening

When you finally arrive at your destination, after a quiet time of study, pen the truths that come alive to you. As you write, more spiritual connections will emerge. You will begin to realize that God has been speaking to you all along. Finally, your ear is tuned to His voice and the lessons He desires to teach you. You draw closer to Him and realize the wooing nature of God is personally drawing you to Him—to know Him better, to understand His nature, and to quicken a deeper thirst inside you for knowing God and His ways. Keep a sabbatical journal. A sample is found below.

My Sabbatical Journey

When all is silent, I feel/hear _____

_____.

Being alone with God makes me feel _____.

Now that I know this about myself, I think God wants me to

_____

Today in nature, God gave me an example of my life. I saw

_____.

I realized _____.

When I finally settled down, I realized _____.

The Scripture I studied today showed me the following things about God's nature:

_____

_____

Meditate on the Five Lessons of Shabbat Rest and Know . . .

What do I now know about God's reliability?

_____

_____

_____

What do I now know about God's majesty?

_____

_____

_____

What do I now know about God's redemption?

_____

_____

What do I now know about God's blessing?

_____

_____

What do I now know about God's sanctification?

_____

_____

As we retreat into the nurturing arms of Jesus Christ, He never fails to reach back, to heal our wounds, and to give us the food we need for our souls. His gracious patience is evident in our lack of finding time alone with Him. So He waits, aware that He knows the answer to our lives' struggles. We only have to take the time to pencil in the Master of the universe. He will give us good gifts, food for the soul, and a new kind of normalcy. He is bigger than we often realize.

Down through the ages, in the midst of our pounding hammers, we find God abiding, working in hearts in spite of us and offering undeserved mercy. As early as Cain, the son of Eve and the first murderer, we see man's drive to build. Cain "went out from the LORD's presence" (Gen 4:16) and built a city, naming it after his son, Enoch. If the story had ended with Cain's lineage, the story of man might have ended altogether.

Wickedness intensified through each generation after Enoch. But Eve bore another son, Seth, whose lineage "began to call on the name of the Lord" (Gen. 4:26). While ambition spread across the earth, so did goodness. Mercy watered goodness, and we see in the life of Seth's descendant, Noah, a different vision for building. He was commanded by God to build an ark, a place of safety from the coming storm that would wash away the corruption spread by man's ambition (see Genesis 7). Herein is the grand contrast: a lineage of ambition that takes evil to deeper and deeper levels and a godly lineage that seeks to know God in deeper ways. The builder versus the trusting heart; man driven versus man resting in God's goodness.

Then we see in the gospel of John a vision of comfort: Christ who smoothes the troubled brow by taking the burden of building upon Himself, the ultimate Ark. He offers a supreme promise to His disciples: "In My Father's house are many mansions; if it were not so, I would have told you. I go to prepare a place for you. And if I go and prepare a place for you, I will come again and receive you to Myself; that where I am, there you may be also" (John 14:2–3 NKJV).

Waiting for that day can be like waiting for a bus in the middle of the Atlantic Ocean. Our hearts grow cold, and we cannot see the day approaching, let alone those ethereal rooftops beyond the clouds. So we pick up the handle of our ambition, pounding against the wood of our earthly hope, and forget the Builder who has already started the greater work—a work that will never weather or rust, built upon the flesh of human hearts.

We know the Scripture so well: "Unless the LORD builds the house, its builders labor in vain. Unless the LORD watches over the city, the watchmen stand guard in vain. In vain you rise early and stay up late, toiling for food to eat—for he grants sleep to those he loves" (Ps. 127:1–2). If only we could see how quickly a work of vanity disintegrates, we might grasp the long-term wisdom of cultivating a rested life.

As I finish writing this last page, I am battling the old ways again. My calendar is filling up, my reading time is drying up, my frustration level is soaring, and my productivity, effectiveness, and joy are sinking in the pit of busyness. A new normal doesn't happen unless pursued; it requires tenacious discipline. New habits don't just maintain a continuous rhythm without our attention; they require outrageous persistence. New standards are easily neglected, slippery, and are often misunderstood by those around us. They are however, worth every ounce of energy required, and repay each ounce expended with renewed enthusiasm and souls capable of bringing healing and producing fruit.

If we can lay down our hammers, our noisemakers, and our plans for a moment, we can hear the music found in the gentle rhythm of rain that lands on the leaf before trickling to earth and know that Jesus is our Living Water. We can listen to the hushing crescendo of wind against the limb and rooftop and remember that God is our covering. From a front porch, we can watch a summer shower build into a dark storm, and witness the almighty power of Christ embedded in the thunder. By reading a Scripture, we can find revealed the architectural rendering for our own lives and know that we are part of something bigger than ourselves.

It all begins by beginning something new and something as normal as the rain. It is a part of our passage, to mark the places where we stop along our journey to listen. We can think of today as the first pile of stones that others will point to like Abram's altars and say, "God did something in this place." Let Him begin that work in the quiet of this moment.

Heavenly Father,

Thank You for teaching me to reflect upon Your higher ways and deeper paths. Show me Your stopping-off places so that I can be fed by Your own hand. Please guide me in the normalcy of Your plan to work hard and then find rest. Let the rhythm of my life's work be in sync with Your own heartbeat. Let Your rest be mine.

In the name of Your Son, Jesus Christ, amen.

My point of dedication: _____

_____

_____

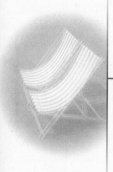

Notes

Chapter 1

1. Anne Morrow Lingberg, *Gift from the Sea* (Vintage Books, 1978), 10.
2. John Ortberg, *The Life You've Always Wanted* (Grand Rapids, MI: Zondervan, 1997),81, 87.
3. Ibid.

Chapter 2

1. John Eldredge, *The Journey of Desire* (Nashville: Thomas Nelson, 2000), 92.
2. Ortberg, *The Life You've Always Wanted*, 155.
3. Anne Lamott, *Bird by Bird* (New York: Anchor Books, published by Doubleday by arangement with Pantheon Books, 1994), 7.
4. Ibid., 27.
5. Jan Winebrenner, *Intimate Faith* (New York: Warner, 2003), 116.
6. Eldredge, *Journey of Desire*, 93.
7. Gary Thomas, *Sacred Pathways* (Grand Rapids, MI: Zondervan, 2000).
8. Philip Yancey, *Reaching for the Invisible God* (Grand Rapids: Harper Collins/ Zondervan, 2002), 183.
9. Wayne Muller, *How Then Shall We Live?* (New York: Bantam Books, 1996).

Chapter 3

1. Jill Briscoe, the entire poem is found in *Heartbeat* (Wheaton: Harold Shaw Publishers, 1991), 9.
2. David Garland, *The NIV Application Commentary: Mark* (Grand Rapids, MI: Zondervan, 1996), 111.
3. Richard J. Foster, *Celebration of Discipline* (San Francisco: HarperCollins, Twentieth Anniv. Ed, 1978, 1988, 1998.), 81.

4. Madeleine L'Engle, *Walking on Water* (Calorado Springs, CO: Shaw, 1972), 152.

5. C.S. Lewis, *Mere Christianity* (NewYork: Macmillan, 1952).

Chapter 4

1. Winebrenner, *Intimate Faith*, 147.

Chapter 6

1. Gerald Sittser, *A Grace Disguised* (Grand Rapids, MI: Zondervan, 1995), 95.

2. Ibid., 99.

3. Billy Graham, *Just As I Am* (San Francisco: HarperCollins, 1997), 138.

4. Ibid., 138–39.

Chapter 7

1. G. K. Chesterton, *Orthodoxy* (Image, 1959) 146.

2. Walt Wangerin, *Ragman: And Other Cries of Faith*, "Preaching," (San Francisco: HarperSanFrancisco, 1984), 81.

Chapter 8

1. Mitch Albom, *Tuesdays with Morrie* (New York:Broadway Books), 70.

2. George Herbert, *The Poetical Works of George Herbert* (New York: D. Appleton and Co., 1857), 52-53.

3. Mount Horeb and Mount Sinai refer to the same mountain, simply different names used by different traditions.

4. Gary Thomas, *Seeking the Face of God* (Eugene, OR: Harvest House, 1994), 105.

5. Ibid., Thomas quoted Pascal from *Pensees*, 48.

6. Alexander Maclaren, *Second Samuel and the Books of Kings, Expositions of Holy Scripture*, vol. 2 (Grand Rapids: Eerdmans, 1952), 261.

Chapter 9

1. Lewis, *Mere Christianity.*, 120

2. Philip Yancey, *What's So Amazing About Grace?* (Harper Collins/Zondervan, 1997), 70.

Chapter 10

1. Anne Lamott, *Traveling Mercies* (Anchor Books, 1999), 118, 119.

2. John Piper, *Brothers, We Are Not Professionals* (Nashville: Broadman & Holman, 2002), 66.

3. Michael Card, *Scribbling in the Sand* (InterVarsity Press, Downers Grove,

IL; Leicester, England, 2003), 92.

4. Yancey, *Reaching for the Invisible God*, 152.

5. Stott's examples are all but nonissues three decades later.

6. Donald G. Bloesch, *The Holy Spirit Works & Gifts* (Downers Grove, IL: InterVarsity, 2000), 48.

7. Donald G. Bloesch, *The Holy Spirit Works and Gifts* (InterVarsity Press, 2000), 37.

8. Ibid.

9. Sereno Dwight, *The Works of Jonathan Edwards*, "The Memoirs of Jonathan Edwards," vol. 1 (Edinburgh: The Banner of Truth Trust, 1974), xx–xxi.

10. Mark Storer, "The Good News According to Twain, Steinbeck, and Dickens," *Christianity Today*, 22 April 2002, 73.

11. John Piper, *Brothers We Are Not Professionals* (Nashville: Broadman & Holman, 2002), 66–67.

12. Ibid., 69–70.

13. Ibid., 90.

14. Donald Whitney, *Spiritual Disciplines for the Christian Life* (Colorado Springs, CO: NavPress, 1991), 195.

15. Maurice Roberts, "Are We Becoming Reformed Men?" *The Banner of Truth*, issue 330, March 1991, 5.

16. Ralph Woods, ed., *A Treasury of the Familiar* (Chicago: People's Book Club, 1945), 14.

17. Whitney, *Spiritual Disciplines for the Christian Life*, 202–3.

18. Bill Hybels, *Too Busy Not to Pray* (Downers Grove, IL: InterVarsity, 1988), 102.

19. Ibid., 103.

20. Ibid.

21. Robert Benson, *Living Prayer* (New York: Tarcher/Putnam, 1999), 175.

22. Ibid., 179.

23. William Kerr, *The Decline of Pleasure* (Simon & Schuster, 1983).

24. Pascal, *Pensees*, (Penguin, 1995), 69.

25. Lindbergh, *Gift from the Sea*, 25–27.

Chapter 12

1. Yancey, *Reaching for the Invisible God*, 231.

2. Ibid.

About the Authors

Pete Briscoe is senior pastor of Bent Tree Bible Fellowship. He is the son of authors/speakers Stuart and Jill Briscoe, and through their guidance learned the dynamics of ministry and church growth. With undergraduate degrees in speech communication, Bible, and political science, Briscoe also holds a Masters of Divinity from Trinity Evangelical Divinity School. He and his wife, Libby, have three children, Cameron, Annika, and Liam.

Award-winning novelist and speaker, **Patricia Hickman** has published fourteen novels, including her critically acclaimed *Fallen Angels* and *Nazareth's Song*. Her works have been praised in such publications as *Publishers Weekly, Romantic Times, Moody Magazine, SHINE Magazine for Women,* and *Library Journal.* Hickman has won two Silver Angel Awards for Excellence in Media and has been a frequent guest nationally on radio programs. Patricia is married and mother to three children—two on earth and one in heaven.

www.patriciahhickman.com

 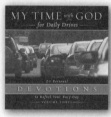

Now you can turn your daily commute into a renewing time with God. Whether you spend several hours a day in traffic or only a few minutes, the *My Time with God for Daily Drives* audio CD provides relief from life's traffic jams and detours.

Each daily reading is 4 minutes or less and steers your heart to God with Scripture, devotional thoughts, and inspirational closings to help you apply Scripture to daily living. It's all set to music and is the perfect way to begin or end your daily commute.

CD Volume One ISBN: 0-7180-0665-8 (Nelson Bibles)

CD Volume Two ISBN: 0-7180-0666-6 (Nelson Bibles)

CD Volume Three ISBN: 0-7180-0861-8 (Nelson Bibles)

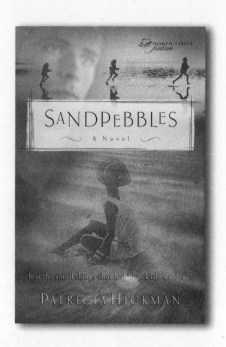

Also by Patricia Hickman, a novel about a young widow who discovers a new lease on life, but only after allowing God to work miracles in her soul.

Recently-widowed March Longfellow efficiently commandeers the lives of her son, Mason, her pastor father, and the staff members of the small-town newspaper she owns, all the while grappling with grief and issues unresolved before her husband's fatal boating accident. When a new pastor comes to town and his family's lives become intertwined with her own, March finds her life thrust into a new direction--one she cannot control. As March begins to release the things of the past, God rekindles her faith and her joy and offers her renewed hope for love.

ISBN: 0-8499-4300-0

WestBow
PRESS

A Division of Thomas Nelson Publishers
Since 1798

visit us at www.westbowpress.com